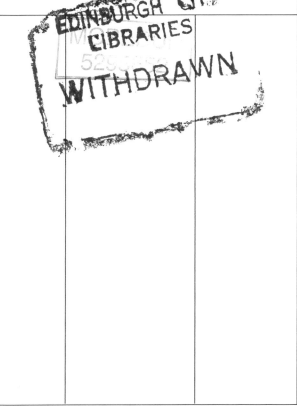

Elly Pear's
Let's Eat!

Elly Pear's
Let's Eat!

Simple, delicious food for everyone, every day

Elly Curshen

Thorsons

Contents

Introduction

Let's Eat! celebrates simple, delicious food. The sort of food I cook day in, day out. Food that brings me joy. It's nutritious (along with some stuff that can barely make claims on the nutrition front but makes me happy). It's centred on vegetables, pulses, grains and dairy with small amounts of fish and seafood. It's inspired by world cooking and the seasons.

This is also, on the whole, quick food. I hate washing up with a passion so I've tried to use as little equipment as possible. I don't have a stand mixer or a microwave or a giant flashy food processor so none of these recipes will require you to have them either. You'll rarely need to put the oven on either – most of these recipes are cooked on the hob. A knife, a chopping board, a mixing bowl, one big saucepan, one small saucepan, a frying pan and a baking tray – that's pretty much it.

It's modern food for the way I live and I hope it fits into your lives too. My two best mates have kids now and spending time with them, cooking together and getting an insight into how this has affected the way they cook, has taught me so much. I think there are lots of recipes here that will be useful if you, too, have the demands of a young family.

My approach to food has been consistent for as long as I can remember – from when I first started cooking as a kid. Deliciousness and joy are my driving force. Texture and flavour, my main concerns. Ease and satisfaction, my aims. None of this has changed, so, add to this useful methods of planning and creating dishes I've picked up along the way, and the result is here...*Let's Eat!*

I am much
more adept at
making dinner
quickly without
sacrificing
deliciousness —
by far the most
important factor
in any meal.

I'm sitting at my kitchen table in Bristol and the last few months have been full of cooking, recipe development, eating, writing, washing up and endless trips to the greengrocer. My thoughts have been dominated by applying the learning from my first book, *Fast Days & Feast Days*, and all my readers' feedback and making this the best, most useful book possible. *Let's Eat!* is the next step for anyone who has enjoyed *Fast Days & Feast Days*, but this book will also stand alone for those of you who didn't buy it. (What the hell? – sort that out right away.)

Although you won't find any recipes labelled as 'fast day' dishes in this book, if you are following the 5:2, you can use the skills you learnt from my first book to calculate the calorie counts, if you want to.* The recipes in the first chapter of this book, with all the various serving suggestions provided, are particularly well suited to this, meaning you can cook for yourself and others at the same time and use a calorie-counted component as part of a bigger meal for all.

*A 'fast day', for those who don't know, is the '2' bit of the 5:2 way of eating – two days a week when you restrict your calorie intake to 500 calories.

I want to show
you how a
little advance
prep can mean
dinner on the
table really
quickly and
easily, any day
of the week.

This has been one of the best bits of feedback from *Fast Days & Feast Days*; following the 5:2 but being able to eat the same food as others is key to keeping the diet up. Who wants to sit and eat a sad 'diet dinner', entirely different from your family or housemates?

While doing the 5:2, I recalibrated my ideas about what it meant to really feel full or hungry. I curbed my tendency to mindlessly eat and got a grip of what a sensible portion size was. I also became much more experienced in finding ways to make dishes more interesting, textured and exciting. My garnish game was strong. Crucially, too, I'd discovered the benefits of batch cooking. I'd started using my freezer for more than ice and peas. I'd sorted out my dry stores and was much more adept at making dinner quickly without sacrificing deliciousness – by far the most important factor in any meal. I'd become an expert in using up bits and pieces after the fast days had created an abundance of half-used packets and produce. Now, I want to show you how a little advance prep can mean dinner on the table really quickly and easily, any day of the week.

How to use *Let's Eat!*

The first chapter of this book contains five freezable batch-cook recipes. Each is accompanied by four recipes to serve up each base in imaginative and wholly different ways, so you're not eating the same thing over and over again.

The second gives you nine building-block recipes, each forming the main component for three delicious dishes – make the base once, serve it three ways. The third and final chapter is full of quick and easy menus – whole curated sets of recipes for all sorts of occasions. It's all covered, from romantic dinners for two to brunch parties and family weeknight dinners. Elements from the previous chapters combined with new recipes and also some bought-in bits. Cook from them as intended, as set menus, or pick and choose individual dishes as you like.

I want to show you some ideas for cookery building blocks that you can then build on in your own way. Lots of inspiration and creative combinations that I hope will get you trying new things, mixing it up and feeling confident to take things in a new direction. These are recipes to make your life easier. Food to be proud of – whether there's anyone else there to see it or not! Let's go. Let's eat.

These are recipes to make your life easier. Food to be proud of – whether there's anyone there to see it or not!

Storecupboard and Staples

There'll be very little in this book that you won't find easily in your local shops or a supermarket.

Apart from fresh produce, the following items are all the things you need to cook the recipes in this book. If there's anything you have trouble sourcing in your neighbourhood, I can't recommend souschef.co.uk highly enough. They won the *Observer Food Monthly* award for Best Independent Retailer. You'll see why. A treasure trove of the world's delights, just a click away.

Storecupboard basics

Oil

I use olive oil for nearly everything – a cheaper one for cooking and fruity, strongly flavoured, top-quality extra-virgin ones for dressings. I keep a cheap vegetable/sunflower oil in stock for deep-frying (straining, cooling and reusing it a couple of times) and love having other interesting things like argan oil or smoked olive oil on hand for using on salads and to dress vegetables while still warm. My (organic, virgin) coconut oil generally lives in my bathroom, where it makes an excellent face cleanser and moisturiser; it only makes occasional forays into my kitchen.

Vinegars

I love the wide variety of vinegars available and they all have their uses. I have shedloads nearby at all times, but the ones I use most frequently are sherry, balsamic, white wine, red wine, apple cider and rice wine.

Other condiments

Mayonnaise, tomato ketchup, Worcestershire sauce, Tabasco, hot sauce, honey, American-style mustard (like French's), English mustard powder, pomegranate molasses, Dijon mustard, wholegrain mustard.

Spices and dried herbs

Bay leaves, cloves, cardamom pods, chilli flakes, coriander seeds, cumin seeds, cinnamon sticks, garam masala, mustard seeds, pul biber (Turkish mild chilli flakes, AKA Aleppo pepper), smoked paprika, star anise, dried thyme, ground cumin, whole nutmeg, vanilla pods, ground cinnamon, Chinese five-spice, turmeric, mixed spice, curry powder, allspice berries, cayenne pepper, chipotle chilli flakes, celery salt, dried oregano.

Nuts and seeds

Blanched almonds, cashew nuts, ground almonds, hazelnuts, nigella seeds, peanuts, pine nuts, pistachios, pumpkin seeds, sesame seeds, sunflower seeds.

Salt and pepper

Black peppercorns in a mill, Maldon sea salt flakes, smoked salt, vanilla salt, pink peppercorns.

Rice and dried pulses

Black beans, red lentils, green lentils, brown rice (short grain is my favourite).

Pasta

If I could only choose two, I'd pick linguine and rigatoni. Hopefully I'll never be called upon to make such a huge decision.

Tins

Coconut milk, tinned tomatoes (chopped, cherry and whole plum), cannellini beans, sweetcorn, chickpeas.

Jars

Pickled jalapeños, passata, pickled turnips, preserved lemons, roasted peppers, capers, olives, chermoula, anchovy fillets. They can live happily on the shelf until opened, then move to the fridge.

Asian ingredients

Miso, udon, thin rice and soba noodles, soy sauce (I use Kikkoman), Sriracha chilli sauce, rice paper wrappers, sesame oil.

Middle Eastern ingredients

Orange blossom water, tahini, sumac, dried rose petals, dried barberries.

Breadcrumbs

I always use fresh breadcrumbs, never the toasted shop-bought kind. Whenever I buy bread I slice it at home, freeze it and then blitz the crusts in a food processor and pop in a freezer bag. Whenever a recipe calls for breadcrumbs, use these.

Other random bits

Vegetable bouillon powder (stock), plain and self-raising flour, caster sugar, both dark and light soft brown sugars, tomato purée, freekeh, giant couscous, sultanas, marmalade, cornflour, dark chocolate, peanut butter, baking powder, porridge oats, instant polenta, cocoa powder, maple syrup, golden syrup, coconut flakes, desiccated coconut, panko breadcrumbs.

Fresh staples

Milk

I always buy organic. It is better in so many ways: for you, the cows, the farmers and the planet (look at organicmilk.co.uk for loads of interesting info), and it only costs a few pence more a pint than non-organic milk. I truly believe it also tastes so much more delicious.

Butter

Butter is something where it really pays to buy the best you can afford. It tastes so much better.

Yoghurt

I use thick Greek-style yoghurt most often and regular natural yoghurt sometimes too. Buy both organic wherever possible.

Eggs

My most used ingredient and I make sure I never run out. Always free-range, organic if you can. Happy chickens lay much nicer eggs. Remember that if you want to poach eggs, they need to be super, super fresh. As they age, the white breaks down inside the shell and you'll find it very difficult to make a neat poached egg.

Bread

Long-life sliced bread makes me feel terrible. Proper, real bread (preferably sourdough) makes me feel happy. Simple as that. I buy a loaf, slice it up and stick it straight in the freezer. No bread ever gets wasted and I toast it straight from frozen. I have been known to buy bread while I'm away on a trip and carry it home in my handbag, slices emerging from my freezer for weeks to come, reminding me of my time away. What better holiday memento is there than one you can eat?

Salad leaves

Buy whole lettuces rather than bags of mixed leaves and wash them as soon as you get them home. Follow these instructions (as we do at The Pear Café) and your lettuce will last at least 4 days...

Buying whole lettuces rather than prepped leaves will save you money, too. We use oakleaf and little gem lettuce at my café, but the same technique works for any lettuce. Fill your sink with ice-cold water. Cut the base off the lettuce, cut out the hardest section of core with the tip of your knife and separate the leaves. Plunge the leaves into the cold water and swish them around with your hand. Transfer to a large bowl, drain the sink and refill with ice-cold water. Rinse the leaves a second time. Take a double handful of leaves and shake them as dry as you can over the sink. Move into a salad spinner and spin really well, pouring away the water every few seconds. The leaves must be totally dry before you continue. Lay a few sheets of kitchen paper inside the largest zip-lock bags you can find. Keeping the leaves whole (cut edges will turn brown quickly), fill the zip-lock bags up to the top, but don't overfill them. Gently lay the bags flat in the bottom of your fridge (or the crisper drawer) and avoid putting anything on top. Change the kitchen paper every day if it looks wet.

Fresh vegetables and fruit

I'm incredibly lucky when it comes to shopping for food in my Bristol neighbourhood. I'm spoilt for choice and have a number of greengrocers within walking distance. I prefer shopping for veg at my local shops rather than in a supermarket for a number of reasons. Supporting local businesses is essential to me but the biggest draw is the selection of produce available. My favourite local grocer's has a brilliant selection and everything is sold loose, so I can buy exactly what I need. Whether it's a single chilli or a lone lemon – supermarkets tend to package things designed for families and that's not how all of us live. If I buy just what I need, I avoid waste and unnecessary expense.

Tofu: lots of people are a bit scared of where to start. What do you look for on the packet? How do you prepare it? What – even – is it?

A beginner's guide to tofu

I use tofu regularly. As I don't eat meat, my protein sources come from elsewhere (mainly lots of pulses, dairy, eggs and tofu), and I've been using various kinds of tofu for years.

Tofu has been around in Asia for over a thousand years, but it's still finding its way into Western kitchens and lots of people are a bit scared of where to start. What do you look for on the packet? How do you prepare it? What. Even. Is it?

The last question is simple to answer. Tofu is just like cheese but is made with soya beans rather than milk. Fresh soya milk is curdled, the curds and whey are separated, and the curds are then pressed into blocks. How firm the tofu is will depend on how much water is pressed out. The blocks are sometimes then smoked, which will make them firmer, as well as obviously giving them a smoky flavour!

Firm

(I like the Organic Smoked Tofu from Dragonfly, which is handmade in Devon.) This is the type you need for the nuggets on page 124. You'll find it in the chiller cabinet in a cardboard box, inside which there's a shrink-wrapped block of tofu with a bit of liquid. Cut open the pack and pour away the water. Sandwich the tofu between a few layers of kitchen roll or a clean tea towel and gently press down for about 20 seconds to get rid of the excess moisture. If you're using it for a stir fry, it won't crisp up until you've got it really dry, so change the paper a few times and press for longer. For the nuggets recipe, you don't need to worry so much as the moisture is actually essential for puffing up the crispy shell.

Smoked and marinated

This sort of tofu is what I call 'beginner's tofu' and you can't go wrong. It also comes in a shrink-wrapped packet but is not at all wet. It can be eaten hot or cold, doesn't need pressing and it has a stronger flavour than plain tofu (so more interesting for those who consider tofu a wobbly, bland blob). I've used this type on page 33 with the lentil dahl. (I like the Taifun brand, the one with almonds and sesame seeds.)

There are two kinds of tofu I regularly buy:

Freeze
f o r
Ease

This chapter contains 25 recipes – five different freezable base recipes, each with four different ways to serve them.

These ways to serve aren't just 'serving suggestions' but proper, full recipes that incorporate the base recipe as a main element. The idea is that you can make big batches of the base but avoid eating the same thing over and over again. The bases are all 'wet' things that freeze well and then defrost and reheat quickly and easily. Some of the ways to use them are casual and perhaps best suited to a weeknight dinner or a speedy lunch when you're just cooking for yourself. Others are smarter and would certainly be up to scratch if you have guests. They're all simple, easy and nothing takes very long. You've invested the time in batch-cooking the base, so the 'serving suggestions' are designed to be quick and stress-free.

If you've got a big enough pot and enough freezer space, you can, of course, double or even triple these recipes. Just don't forget to alter your cooking times accordingly.

So, equip yourself with plenty of plastic tubs and a permanent marker to label everything, stick the radio on, grab a drink and let's cook!

Lentil, tomato and coconut dhal

recipe overleaf

Lentil, tomato and coconut dhal

Learn how to make a dhal (a lentil-based curry) and you are opening up a whole world of nutritious, delicious, cheap meals. It is quick to make, so you can whip this up from scratch after work even if you've not had time to batch-cook in advance. All the warming spices make this 'spiced' (think fragrant and aromatic) not 'spicy' (think chilli heat). Add extra chilli flakes if you like it hot.

I've used whole tinned plum tomatoes in this one, to add a nice contrast in texture. You can use a ready-made garam masala spice blend or make your own. Either way, make sure your spices are fresh and not from an open packet, shoved in the back of your cupboard, six years out-of-date. Mentioning no names.

Makes 6 portions
(approx. 460g each)

—

4 tbsp oil (vegetable, sunflower,
    olive or coconut) or ghee
2 medium onions, peeled and
    finely diced
5cm piece of root ginger
    (approx. 30g), peeled and
    grated or finely chopped
3 garlic cloves, peeled and grated
    or finely chopped
3 tsp vegetable bouillon powder
2 tbsp garam masala (make
    your own, see below, or buy)
1–2 tsp chilli flakes, to taste
2 tbsp black mustard seeds
500g red lentils, rinsed
2 x 400g tins plum tomatoes
1 x 400g tin coconut milk
flaked sea salt and freshly
    ground black pepper

Garam masala
2 tsp coriander seeds
2 tsp cumin seeds
1 cinnamon stick
4 cloves
½ tsp black peppercorns
4 cardamom pods
2 star anise
2 bay leaves

Heat the oil in a large saucepan over a medium-low heat, add the onion, ginger, garlic and a big pinch of flaked sea salt and cook for 10 minutes until softened but not coloured, stirring occasionally.

Meanwhile, if you're making your own garam masala, toast the ingredients in a dry pan over a low heat for 1–2 minutes until smelling fantastic, keeping the spices moving. Tip into a pestle and mortar or spice grinder and grind to a fine powder.

Dissolve the bouillon powder in 1 litre of boiling water for the stock. Add the garam masala, chilli flakes and mustard seeds to the onion mixture in the saucepan, stir thoroughly, then add the lentils. Give everything a good mix. Add the tomatoes and the stock and bring to the boil. Turn the heat down to low and cook for 20–25 minutes until the lentils are tender and retain no bite, stirring frequently and deeply so the lentils don't stick and crushing the tomatoes a bit as you go. Add the coconut milk, remove from the heat and season to taste with flaked sea salt and pepper.

To freeze
Divide the dhal evenly between 6 sealable containers or freezer bags and leave to cool completely at room temperature. Label each portion with the recipe name and date made, then place in the freezer and use within 3 months. Defrost in the fridge (it will take approximately 8 hours to defrost), then gently reheat in a saucepan over a medium-low heat until piping hot.

To chill
The dhal will be fine for 3 days in the fridge. Keep it covered and when you are ready to reheat, gently simmer in a saucepan over a medium-low heat until piping hot. Adding a squeeze of lemon before you plate it up is a nice idea too.

As a soup with roasted peppers and toasted cashews

Serves 6

—

2 portions of Lentil, Tomato and
    Coconut Dhal (see recipe,
    pages 26–7)
1 x 450g jar roasted red peppers,
    drained and roughly chopped,
    (350g drained weight)
1 tsp vegetable bouillon powder
1 small handful of cashew nuts
2 naan breads, to serve (optional)

Two portions of dhal turn into six portions of soup, with the simple addition of a jar of roasted red peppers and some stock. You could swap the cashews for any other toasted nuts or seeds, but I think the creamy cashews work particularly well with the spiced soup.

Tip the dhal into a large saucepan, add the chopped roasted peppers and place over a medium heat. Add the bouillon powder and 400ml boiling water and bring to a simmer.

Meanwhile, toast the cashews in a dry pan over a medium heat for 1–2 minutes until golden brown, shaking the pan often. Remove from the heat and roughly chop.

Remove the dhal from the heat and blitz with a hand-held or stand blender until smooth.

Pour into bowls and top with the toasted cashews. Serve with the naan breads (if using).

With a 6-minute egg and toasted breadcrumbs

The dhal heats up in exactly the same time as the egg takes to cook. It's like the universe wanted them to be together in the bowl. The silky egg yolk and the creamy dhal are shouting out for some crunchy texture, however, and these toasted breadcrumbs are exactly what you need. I rarely cook with coconut oil but I think it works really well here. The nutty toasted crumbs on top of the egg and dhal is a frugal, simple, delicious and quick supper. Pretty perfect.

Serves 1
—

1 free-range egg
1 portion of Lentil, Tomato and
    Coconut Dhal (see recipe,
    pages 26–7)
1 tsp olive oil or coconut oil
10g fresh breadcrumbs
1 tbsp chopped coriander
    leaves (optional)
¼ red chilli, finely sliced (optional)

Make sure the egg is at room temperature. Fill a small saucepan with boiling water and bring to a continuous boil over a medium heat – this is for the egg. Stick the dhal in another small saucepan and place over a medium-low heat until piping hot; stir occasionally.

Gently lower the egg into the boiling water and immediately set your timer for 6 minutes. While the egg cooks, heat the oil in a small frying pan, add the breadcrumbs and toast for about 1 minute until golden brown, shaking the pan often. Remove from the heat and keep to one side.

When the timer goes off, remove both pans from the heat. Pour away the hot water, holding your egg back with a spoon. Sit the (now dry) pan in the sink and turn the cold tap on, blasting the egg until totally cold. Roll the egg on the counter, pressing down gently, until the shell cracks all over. Peel very carefully and use a very sharp knife to cut it in half, lengthways.

Put the dhal into a bowl, sit the egg on top and sprinkle over the breadcrumbs, chopped coriander and sliced chilli (if using, which you totally should), then serve.

With wilted greens, lemon and yoghurt

I adore spring greens. They've been 99p for a huge bag in my greengrocer's for as long as I can remember. Does inflation not affect greens? I take off the outside leaves if they're grotty and then cut the whole cabbage up into ribbons, widthways. Dump them in a sinkful of water, as hot as a bath, and swish them around a bit. When they hit the butter in the pan, they'll already be half-cooked.

Serves 1

—

25g salted butter
1 lemon, ½ juiced, ½ left whole
1 big handful of chopped spring greens or any other greens you like (approx. 250g)
1 portion of Lentil, Tomato and Coconut Dhal (see recipe, pages 26–7)
1 heaped tbsp Greek-style yoghurt
1 pinch of pul biber (mild Turkish chilli flakes)
½ spring onion, finely sliced
flaked sea salt

Melt the butter in a medium saucepan over a low heat, along with the juice of half a lemon. Wash the greens but do not shake dry, then add to the pan, along with a big pinch of flaked sea salt. Cover with a lid and cook over a medium heat for a few minutes until al dente, stirring occasionally.

Meanwhile, reheat the dhal in a small saucepan over a medium-low heat until piping hot, stirring occasionally.

Put the warmed dhal into a bowl and using tongs, add the buttery, lemony greens. Add a dollop of yoghurt and sprinkle with the pul biber flakes and sliced spring onion. Wedge of lemon on the side and you're done.

With seared tofu, avocado, pickles and seeds

Smoked, marinated tofu is what I would call 'beginners' tofu' – you can't screw it up (see page 19). It doesn't need pressing, it is ready to eat (hot or cold) and it is already flavoured by the smoking, so if you've never cooked with tofu, here is where you should start. All those benefits mean it is a bit more expensive than other tofus, so once you've tried it, move on to other types and learn how to use them. There's a whole world of tofu out there!

Serves 2
—

2 portions of Lentil, Tomato and Coconut Dhal (see recipe, pages 26–7)
1 tbsp mixed seeds (pumpkin, sunflower, sesame, poppy and nigella)
1 tbsp olive oil, ghee or coconut oil
1 x 200g packet of smoked marinated tofu, sliced (see my guide to tofu, page 19)
1 ripe avocado
a few pickles (any kind, homemade or shop-bought. Middle Eastern pickled turnips are particularly good for this)

Reheat the dhal in a small saucepan over a medium-low heat until piping hot, stirring occasionally.

Meanwhile, toast the seeds in a dry frying pan over a medium heat until starting to burst, shaking the pan often, then tip into a bowl and return the pan to the heat. Add the oil and turn the heat up to high. Once hot, add the tofu slices and cook for a couple of minutes until browned on both sides.

Peel, stone and slice the avocado. Stick the hot dhal in a bowl, add the tofu slices, avocado and pickles, then sprinkle over the toasted seeds.

Mean feat no-meat meatballs

recipe overleaf

Mean feat no-meat meatballs

I wanted to create a veggie meatball recipe that would be really versatile. The flavourings go well with Italian-style dishes like the first two serving suggestions, but are also happy in a more Middle Eastern setting (inside a wrap with hummous and lots of fragrant toppings) or made into a burger with my mate Dan's special Fry Sauce.

By the way, I tried frying them and they fell apart. Baked on an oiled tray, they cooked evenly and stayed perfectly spherical. So, learn from my experience. Baked balls. Now, that's an alternative title idea...

Makes 22 balls
—

2 tbsp olive oil, plus extra
for greasing
1 aubergine, cut into 3cm chunks
½ tsp chilli flakes
1 heaped tsp chopped
rosemary leaves
1 heaped tbsp chopped
flat-leaf parsley leaves
½ tsp hot smoked paprika
1 lemon, zested
1 onion (approx. 100g), peeled
and finely diced
1 garlic clove, peeled and crushed
or finely grated
75g fresh breadcrumbs
flaked sea salt and freshly ground
black pepper

Heat 1 tablespoon of the oil in a large frying pan over a medium-high heat. Add the aubergine chunks and 3 tablespoons of water. Season and cook for 10 minutes until browned, stirring occasionally. Meanwhile, put the chilli flakes, rosemary, parsley, paprika and lemon zest into a food processor.

Tip the cooked aubergine into the food processor and wipe out the pan with kitchen paper. Return to a low heat. Heat the remaining tablespoon of oil, add the onion and the garlic and fry for 5–7 minutes. Tip into the food processor and blitz everything into a rough purée. Add the breadcrumbs and blitz again. Chill in the fridge for at least 20 minutes.

Line a baking tray with foil and lightly grease. Wet your hands and roll the mixture into 22 ping-pong-sized balls. Now, lay them on the lined tray, cover them with cling film and leave in the fridge or freezer until you're ready to cook. The following recipes require the balls to be uncooked but you can cook them straight away and eat as you like. Simply preheat the oven to 180°C/350°F/Gas mark 4 and bake the tray of meatballs in the hot oven for 30–35 minutes.

To freeze
Lay the balls on a tray, cover with cling film and place in the freezer until frozen. You can then tip them into a freezer bag. Label with the recipe name and the date made, then place in the freezer and use within 3 months. Defrost in the fridge; overnight is fine, or take them out in the morning and they'll be defrosted once you're ready to make dinner.

To chill
If you don't want to freeze them, the balls are fine, uncooked, for 3 days in the fridge. Keep them covered, then, when ready to eat them, bake as above.

In a wrap with hummous, soft herbs, toasted pine nuts and yoghurt

I've not included exact quantities for the toppings because it's really up to you. Use all or some of these, pile up as much as you like and make your own Wrap of Dreams. Cooling yoghurt and some sort of hot sauce are pretty essential in my opinion and I love to use loads of herbs, almost as a salad rather than a garnish. Swap hummous for aïoli (see recipe, page 54) if you've made some and, if you're really hungry, add a couple of slices of seared halloumi to make this even better!

Serves 1

—

olive oil, for greasing
3 uncooked Mean Feat No-meat
    Meatballs (see recipe, pages
    36–7)
1 tsp pine nuts
1 large flatbread, wrap or pitta bread
a dollop of hummous
a couple of leaves of little gem
    lettuce, shredded
a dollop of natural yoghurt
1 tbsp chopped mint,
    coriander and flat-leaf
    parsley leaves
pomegranate molasses and/or chilli
    sauce, for drizzling (optional)

Preheat the oven to 180°C/350°F/Gas mark 4.

Line a baking tray with foil and grease with the olive oil. Stick the meatballs on the tray and cook in the hot oven for 30–35 minutes.

When the balls are nearly done, toast the pine nuts in a dry frying pan over a medium heat for 1–2 minutes until golden brown, shaking the pan often. Tip into a bowl and return the pan to the heat. Warm the flatbread, wrap or pitta through in the pan on both sides. Smear the hummous over the middle of the flatbread or wrap (if using a pitta, carefully slice open and spread the hummous inside). Pile the shredded lettuce onto the flatbread or wrap, or stuff into the pitta. Remove the balls from the oven and sit on top of the lettuce. Add the yoghurt, top with the chopped herbs and toasted pine nuts, drizzle with a little pomegranate molasses or chilli sauce (if using), then roll up and shove in your face.

With tomato-butter sauce and pasta

I found a pasta shape called 'fusilli lunghi bucati' when I first made this dish and it's the most ridiculous thing: very thin, tightly curled tubes, about 60cm long. If you can find it, I highly recommend it for a bit of fun, but I think linguine or spaghetti would be my next choice.

The sauce is based on the famous Marcella Hazan recipe for tomato sauce. Whereas Hazan discards the onion half before serving, I like to keep the onion and blitz the whole lot. Don't reduce the amount of butter. You'll thank me.

Serves 2

—

1 x 400g tin plum tomatoes
50g salted butter
½ onion, peeled, unchopped
6–10 uncooked Mean Feat No-meat Meatballs (see recipe, pages 36–7), depending on how hungry you are
pasta (spaghetti, linguine, fettucine…whatever kind you like and as much as you want)
2 tsp extra-virgin olive oil, plus extra for greasing
flaked sea salt and freshly ground black pepper
a few fresh basil leaves, to serve
finely chopped rosemary leaves, to serve
Parmesan cheese, to serve

Preheat the oven to 180°C/350°F/Gas mark 4. Line a baking tray with foil and grease with a little olive oil.

To make the sauce, tip the whole tin of tomatoes into a small saucepan. Add the butter, the onion half (unchopped) and a big pinch of flaked sea salt. Place over a medium heat until it starts to blip, then turn the heat right down. Cook for 45 minutes, uncovered, stirring occasionally and mashing up the tomato with the back of a spatula.

After the sauce has been cooking for a few minutes, stick the meatballs on the lined tray and bake in the hot oven for 30–35 minutes. While the meatballs are baking in the oven and the sauce is bubbling away, cook the pasta according to the packet instructions.

After the sauce has been cooking for 45 minutes, use a hand-held blender to blitz the whole lot, onion and all.

Drain the pasta, drizzle with the olive oil and place on plates or in shallow bowls. Place the cooked balls on top and cover the whole lot with sauce.

Sprinkle over the herbs, grate over some Parmesan and season with lots of black pepper … use any or all of these to make it just how you like it. Devour.

Squished into a burger, in a bun with Dan's Fry Sauce

One of my biggest peeves as a non-meat eater is restaurants thinking that if you want a burger, you want a wholemeal bun and none of the good stuff. If I want a burger I want it ALL, just not the meat. I want cheese (there's a time and place for sliced cheese and it's here and now), I want pickles, I want lettuce and I want plenty of sauce. My mate Dan created this 'Fry Sauce' recipe. Originating in Utah, this is used as a sauce in burgers, as a dip for fries and even as a dressing for salad. The standard version is simply one part ketchup to two parts mayonnaise (so that's basically prawn cocktail sauce, right?), but most burger joints have their own closely guarded recipes, with additional bits. Inspired, Dan knocked up his own version, which is, as he would say, 'frigging superb'. Tangy and spicy, yet smooth.

Serves 4

—

2 tsp olive oil, plus extra for greasing
12 uncooked Mean Feat No-meat
    Meatballs (see recipe, pages
    36–7)
4 burger buns
a few leaves of little gem
    lettuce, shredded
½ red onion, peeled and finely diced
2 dill pickles, sliced
4 slices of burger cheese
4 portions of chips, to serve (optional)

For the Fry Sauce
1 tbsp French's classic yellow mustard
1½ tbsp Heinz ketchup
2 heaped tbsp Hellman's mayonnaise
1 tsp Colman's English mustard
2 heaped tbsp finely chopped
    gherkins or cornichons
2 dashes of Tabasco
1 dash of Worcestershire sauce
freshly ground black pepper

Preheat the oven to 180°C/350°F/Gas mark 4.

Line a baking tray with foil, grease with a little olive oil and set to one side. Use wet hands to combine 3 of the Mean Feat No-meat Meatballs to make 1 burger patty. Repeat until you have 4 patties. Place the patties on the lined tray, use your finger to brush the tops with the oil, and place in the oven to cook for 30–35 minutes, turning halfway through. You could stick some chips in the oven at the same time. I won't stop you.

While the burgers are cooking, make the sauce. Just mix everything together in a small bowl with a pinch of black pepper. That's it. Set to one side and toast the buns cut-side down in a dry frying pan over a medium heat until lightly golden.

Assemble the burgers. I'd suggest: Fry sauce on the base bun, lettuce, onion, pickles, burger, cheese, more sauce, top bun. But it's up to you.

Baked with tomatoes, basil and lemon ricotta

The balls nestle into the cherry tomato sauce and dollops of cool, lemony ricotta fill the gaps. The tops of the balls crisp up as they bake, while their hidden bottoms stay soft. Delicious. You could swap the ricotta for torn-up mozzarella or even bits of feta. Keep the lemon zest though – it really lifts the dish. This is a real crowd-pleaser and I'm sure you're going to end up making it loads…

Serves 2

—

1 tbsp olive oil, plus extra for greasing
½ onion, peeled and finely diced
1 garlic clove, peeled and crushed
    or finely grated
½ tsp chilli flakes
2 tbsp tomato purée
1 x 400g tin cherry tomatoes
    in tomato juice
1 small handful of basil leaves,
    plus a few extra, to serve
½ tsp sugar
6–10 uncooked Mean Feat No
    Meat Meatballs, depending
    on how hungry you are (see
    recipe, pages 36–7)
6 tbsp ricotta
1 lemon, zested
flaked sea salt and freshly ground
    black pepper
a few slices of quality bread, to serve
crisp green salad, to serve

Preheat the oven to 180°C/350°F/Gas mark 4.

Heat the oil in a saucepan over a medium heat. Add the onion and garlic and cook for 5–7 minutes, or until translucent. Add the chilli flakes and the tomato purée and cook for a further 1–2 minutes. Add the tinned tomatoes, handful of basil leaves and sugar and season well with flaked sea salt and black pepper. Bring to the boil, then turn the heat down to low and simmer for 20 minutes.

Meanwhile, grease the base of a baking dish with a little olive oil and sit the balls in, evenly spaced. Stick in the hot oven for 20 minutes while the sauce cooks.

After the sauce has been cooking for 15 minutes, check the seasoning then remove the baking dish from the oven and pour the sauce over and around the balls. Mix the ricotta with the lemon zest and spoon little teaspoonfuls of lemony ricotta into the spaces between the balls. Drizzle the whole lot with a little olive oil and stick it back in the oven for another 20 minutes.

Remove from the oven, top with the remaining basil leaves and serve with crusty bread/garlicky toasts or a crisp green salad. Or both.

TIP

Spoon any leftover ricotta onto softly scrambled eggs, sprinkle with chives and serve with hot buttered toast.

More recipes to use up ricotta on pages 43, 50 and 112

Tuscan-style cannellini bean stew

recipe overleaf

Tuscan-style cannellini bean stew

This stew is especially great on chilly days but as it uses really basic veg that are available all year round, you don't need to keep it for the depths of winter; the same recipe made with sweet spring veg would be wonderful. Although I think cannellini beans work best for this, you could swap them for butter beans or chickpeas, or even use a mixture. Don't rush the first section. The finely diced veg (known as *mirepoix* in Chef Speak AKA French) need to be cooked over a low-medium heat for the full 10 minutes so they're sweet and tender before you add everything else.

Makes 8 portions
(approx. 400g each)

—

4 tbsp olive oil
2 small onions, peeled and
    finely diced
3 medium carrots, peeled
    and diced
3 celery sticks, trimmed, cut
    into 2.5cm sections, fat bits
    halved lengthways
8 garlic cloves, peeled and
    crushed or grated
4 x 400g tins cannellini beans,
    drained and rinsed,
    (960g drained weight)
4 tsp vegetable bouillon powder
1 heaped tbsp roughly chopped
    sage leaves
1 heaped tbsp thyme leaves
1 heaped tbsp finely chopped
    rosemary leaves
2 x 400g tins chopped tomatoes
flaked sea salt and freshly ground
    black pepper

Heat the olive oil in a large saucepan over a low heat. Add the onion and cook for a couple of minutes, stirring often. Add the carrot, celery and garlic and cook for a further 10 minutes. Meanwhile, fill and boil the kettle.

Add the drained beans, 1½ litres of boiling water, the bouillon powder, herbs and tinned tomatoes. Season with sea salt and black pepper, stir, bring to the boil, then turn the heat down to low and simmer for 30–45 minutes until the celery and carrot are tender, stirring occasionally.

To freeze
Divide the stew evenly between 8 sealable containers or freezer bags and leave to cool completely at room temperature. Label each portion with the recipe name and the date made, then place in the freezer and use within 3 months. Defrost in the fridge (it will take approximately 8 hours to defrost), then gently reheat in a saucepan over a medium-low heat until piping hot.

To chill
The stew will be fine for 3 days in the fridge. Keep it covered and when you are ready to reheat, gently simmer in a saucepan over a medium-low heat until piping hot.

With a three-cheese toastie

There are three things that will up your toastie game considerably: 1) buttering the outside of your bread; 2) using a mixture of cheeses; 3) pressing down evenly so all the bread is in contact with the hot pan. Do all these things and thank me later.

Serves 1

—

2 tsp salted butter
2 slices of sourdough bread
25g mature Cheddar cheese, grated
1 heaped tbsp ricotta
1 heaped tsp Parmesan cheese,
    freshly grated
1 spring onion, finely sliced
1 portion of Tuscan-style
    Cannellini Bean Stew (see
    recipe, pages 48–9)
flaked sea salt and freshly ground
    black pepper

Start by placing a dry frying pan over a high heat or preheating a sandwich press. You want it really hot.

Butter the slices of bread on what will be the outside of the sandwich. Mix the cheeses together in a small bowl, along with the spring onion, a pinch of sea salt and black pepper. Spread the mixture onto one of the slices of bread and close the sandwich.

Reheat the stew in a saucepan over a medium-low heat until piping hot, stirring occasionally.

Place the sandwich on the hot plate of the sandwich press or, if you're using a frying pan, put it in the pan then use a pan lid to press down quite hard and evenly, so the whole surface of the sandwich is in contact with the heat. After approximately 5 minutes – when the sandwich is really nice and golden – flip over.

When the sandwich is cooked on both sides and the stew is hot, pour the stew into a mug or bowl, put the sandwich on a board and sprinkle both with flaked sea salt. Slice the sandwich in half and eat, being careful not to burn your lip!

As a soup with pesto

The stew lends itself really well to the addition of a bright swirl of punchy pesto. I've done a non-traditional mix here using hazelnuts and sunflower seeds instead of pine nuts and a mixture of basil and sage. Of course, feel free to chuck a dollop of shop-bought pesto in if you have no inclination to make your own right now. I've blitzed half the stew up and kept half chunky so you get a nice halfway texture. Go full smooth or full chunky if you'd prefer.

Serves 4

—

4 portions of Tuscan-style
    Cannellini Bean Stew (see recipe,
    pages 48–9)
flaked sea salt and freshly ground
    black pepper

For the pesto (use good-quality
shop-bought or…):
25g hazelnuts
25g sunflower seeds
1 large handful of basil leaves
6 sage leaves
25g Parmesan cheese, freshly grated
3 tbsp olive oil
½ garlic clove, peeled

Tip 2 of the portions of stew into a saucepan and use a hand-held blender to blitz until smooth. Add the remaining two portions and simmer over a medium-low heat until piping hot, adding a little boiling water if you'd prefer a thinner soup. Season to taste with flaked sea salt and black pepper.

Meanwhile, make the pesto by toasting the nuts and seeds in a dry pan over a medium heat for 1–2 minutes until golden, shaking the pan often.

Put the toasted nuts and seeds along with the remaining pesto ingredients in a mini-blender and whizz until it is as smooth as you like it – it's quite nice left pretty chunky for this.

When the soup is hot, pour into bowls and swirl a spoonful of the pesto on the surface.

With cavolo nero and gremolata

Add ribbons of cavolo nero to the bean stew and you've basically made the Italian peasant style soup/stew called ribollita, just without the traditional bread element. Tear some chunks of good stale bread and throw them in with the greens to really bulk this up, if you fancy going the whole hog. As I'm not doing much hard manual labour out in the fields, I find the beans are filling enough without the bread. The gremolata is a quick and easy way to really add loads of bright flavour to the stew.

Serves 2
—

2 portions of Tuscan-style Cannellini Bean Stew (see recipe, pages 48–9)
100g cavolo nero, shredded

For the gremolata
1 tsp extra-virgin olive oil
1 lemon, zested
1 garlic clove, peeled and finely chopped
1 tbsp chopped flat-leaf parsley leaves

Reheat the stew in a saucepan over a medium-low heat, stirring occasionally. After a couple of minutes, add the cavolo nero and simmer for a further 15 minutes.

Meanwhile, to make the gremolata, mix the oil, lemon zest, garlic and parsley together.

Once the stew is hot, pour into shallow bowls and sprinkle the gremolata over the top.

With crispy-skinned fish and aïoli

I was in two minds about including this recipe for aïoli. It's a little challenging, there's no denying it. It can go a bit wrong and 'split', BUT, learning how to fix the issue and nailing it is one of the kitchen's most satisfying skills. Mayo from a jar is a different beast to homemade. It's really worth giving this a go. It might not feel like it while your arm is killing from whisking but as you drape a silky dollop of homemade aïoli across the fish, you'll glow with pride. Go for it.

Serves 2

—

2 portions of Tuscan-style Cannellini Bean Stew (see recipe, pages 48–9)
olive oil
2 fillets of firm white fish, approx. 150–250g each (sea bass, sea bream, cod, hake are all great choices)
6–10 sage leaves

For the aïoli (use good-quality shop-bought or...)
1 free-range egg yolk
135ml rapeseed oil
2–3 tsp freshly squeezed lemon juice
¼ tsp mustard powder
½–1 garlic clove, peeled and grated or crushed
flaked sea salt

> You can make the aïoli in advance; it will keep for 3 days covered in the fridge. Try splitting the mayo batch in half, then adding garlic to one half and herbs to the other. Tarragon works really well for this.

If you are going for the homemade aïoli, start with this. Make sure all the ingredients are at room temperature first. Place a damp tea towel beneath a bowl and put in the egg yolk. Beat well with a balloon whisk for a couple of minutes. Add a generous pinch of sea salt and beat well for another 30 seconds. Pour in the oil drop by drop, whisking continuously. This stage should take about 10 minutes in total. You really mustn't rush it otherwise the mayonnaise will split. However, if it does split, a tiny splash (half a teaspoon, max) of ice-cold water does miracles in bringing it back to life. Once the aïoli is thick and glossy and the consistency is to your liking (you might not end up using all of the oil), add the lemon juice, mustard powder and garlic, mix well and keep to one side.

Reheat the 2 portions of stew in a saucepan over a medium-low heat until piping hot, stirring occasionally. To cook the fish, heat a glug of olive oil in a frying pan over a high heat. Pat the fish dry and make 2mm-deep slashes into the skin 2–3 times, then sprinkle with salt. Carefully lay the fillets in the hot pan, skin-side down, and press down with a spatula for about 30 seconds. Release and leave to cook for 3–5 minutes until the skin is crisp. Do not move the fish during this time.

cont.

Carefully flip over and cook for a further 2–5 minutes, depending on thickness. To check the fish is cooked, poke a small, sharp knife into the thickest part of the fish – it should go in easily and feel hot to the touch. Throw the sage leaves into the frying pan to crisp up during the last 30 seconds. Pour the hot stew into shallow bowls, top with the fish, a dollop of aïoli and sprinkle with the crispy sage.

Black beans
– refried
if you like

recipe overleaf

Black beans – refried if you like

Black beans (sometimes called turtle beans) have a fantastic rich flavour and velvety texture and they hold their shape well during cooking. They are incredibly high in fibre and protein and ridiculously cheap, especially if you use dried beans.

The recipe is split into two. First you cook dried black beans from scratch, then, if you want to go a step further, you can 'refry' them. Any of the following recipes will work with either the simply cooked beans, the refried beans or a tin of shop-bought refried beans, but I recommend the refrying-yourself method as by far the most delicious.

Makes 12 portions
(approx. 100g each)

—

2 tbsp olive oil
1 medium onion, peeled and
    finely diced
2 garlic cloves, peeled and
    crushed or grated
500g dried black beans, soaked
    overnight in plenty of cold water,
    then drained
2 tsp dried thyme
flaked sea salt

To make 4 x 250g portions of
refried beans
40g salted butter (or olive oil if you
    want to keep them vegan)
1 onion, peeled and diced
½ tsp bouillon powder
1 tsp ground cumin
½ tsp chilli powder
½ tsp smoked paprika
2½ portions cooked black beans
    (250g) or 1 x 400g tin cooked
    black beans, drained and rinsed
    (230g drained weight)
½–1 tsp flaked sea salt
2 tbsp chopped coriander
    leaves, to serve

You can also buy a tin of
refried beans and carry on
with any of the following
4 recipes using those. It's
OK. Remember, though,
if you make it yourself, it's
lots cheaper and you can
control the spice level and
the salt content.

Heat the oil in a large saucepan over a low heat, add the onion, cover and fry for 5 minutes until softened. Stir in the garlic. Add the beans and thyme, then cover with cold water, plus 2cm more. Bring to the boil, reduce the heat and gently simmer for 1 hour, uncovered, stirring occasionally and topping up the water if needed.

Once the beans have softened, drain and season with plenty of flaked sea salt. Save the cooking liquid to thin down your refried beans, if needed. The beans are now ready to be used as they are or you can 'refry' them … (which is slightly misleading as you're not frying them twice, you are boiling them and then frying them. Confusing).

To 'refry' the beans, melt the butter in a large pan over a medium-low heat and soften the onion for 5 minutes until translucent, stirring often. Meanwhile, dissolve the bouillon powder in 125ml of boiling water for the stock.

Add the cumin, chilli and paprika to the onions and stir to coat. Add the beans and stock, stir well, then remove from the heat and mash the beans. Keep the mixture as chunky or as smooth as you like – I like it with a few rogue whole beans poking through. If the mixture is too loose, reduce the liquid until thickened over a medium-high heat, then season to taste.

To freeze
Divide the beans evenly between 12 sealable containers or freezer bags and cool completely at room temperature. Label each portion with the recipe name and date made, then place in the freezer and use within 3 months. Defrost in the fridge; overnight is fine, or take them out in the morning so they are defrosted by dinner time. Then just refry before serving.

To chill
The beans will be fine for up to 3 days in the fridge, covered. To reheat, gently simmer over a medium-low heat until piping hot. Serve with chopped coriander.

Baked with green rice and eggs

A bright green, fragrant, spiced, herby rice hides at the bottom of this dish, layered up and baked with refried beans, chopped tomatoes and eggs. The surface is then covered with avocado, toasted seeds and hot sauce. All the good stuff. You're going to love this one. Make a mini-one for yourself with leftovers and just one egg in a little ramekin, or scale it up and feed a crowd, like in the photograph.

Serves 2

—

200g cooked rice (I prefer short grain brown but use whichever rice you prefer)
butter, for greasing
500g Black Beans – Refried If You Like (see recipe, pages 58–9)
175g ripe mixed-colour cherry tomatoes, quartered
2 free-range eggs (or more if you're hungry)
1 heaped tbsp pumpkin seeds
½ ripe avocado
hot sauce, to serve

For the green paste
1 bunch of coriander (approx. 30g)
2 spring onions, roughly chopped
2 level tbsp pickled jalapeño slices, drained
25g cavolo nero or kale, roughly chopped
2 garlic cloves, peeled and chopped
1 tbsp vegetable or olive oil
flaked sea salt

Preheat the oven to 180°C/350°F/Gas mark 4.

Pick a small handful of coriander leaves, roughly chop and set aside to use later. To make the green paste, roughly chop the remaining the coriander, stalks and all, and put into a food processor with the rest of the green paste ingredients and a pinch of flaked sea salt. Blitz until you have a rough mixture. If you don't have a food processor, chop the ingredients as finely as you can and mix with the oil.

Tip the cooked rice into a bowl, add the green paste and mix until evenly combined.

Grease the base and sides of a 20 x 15cm oven dish with butter. Spoon the rice mixture into the dish and spread into an even layer. Spread the refried beans on top, then scatter with the cherry tomatoes. Use the back of a spoon to make two dents in the surface and crack in the eggs.

Pop the dish in the hot oven for 25–30 minutes until the egg whites are just set. Meanwhile, toast the seeds in a dry frying pan over a medium heat for 1–2 minutes until starting to burst, shaking the pan often, and then remove from the heat. Peel, stone and slice the avocado. When the eggs are done, remove the dish from the oven, top with avocado, coriander and toasted pumpkin seeds, add a shake of hot sauce to serve.

This recipe is really easily scalable, whether you want to make a dish for one or a family-sized meal. Just keep the layers (green rice, then beans, tomatoes, then eggs), and the rough proportions the same.

You need to use cooked rice for this recipe so cook the rice before you start. You could of course buy one of those sachets of cooked rice if you really want to.

I have a hashtag on
Instagram solely for ideas to
use up that bag of kale in the
fridge, so there's no excuse
to waste any!

#100 ways with kale

As part of huevos rancheros

There's lots of versions of this Mexi-style breakfast out there and mine is based on a dish at one of my fave Bristol places, Bakers and Co on Gloucester Road. I love their fresh crunchy cucumber salsa which provides amazing contrast with the spiced, hot refried beans. I keep the tortilla back until I've finished everything else and then use it to wipe the plate.

Serves 1
—

250–500g Black Beans – Refried If You Like (see recipe, pages 58–9), depending on hunger levels
6 ripe cherry tomatoes, roughly chopped
½ tsp finely chopped fresh red chilli (optional)
1 small wedge of onion, peeled and very finely diced
2 tbsp finely diced cucumber
1 tbsp roughly chopped coriander leaves, plus a few extra leaves to garnish
½ tsp apple cider or white wine vinegar
olive or vegetable oil
1–2 free-range eggs, depending on hunger levels
1 soft tortilla
1 wedge of lime, to serve
flaked sea salt and freshly ground black pepper
hot sauce, to serve

Swap the raw cherry tomatoes for roasted if you prefer. Use a corn rather than flour tortilla for a gluten-free alternative, or replace the egg with some avocado to make this a vegan dish.

Reheat the beans in a small pan over a low heat until piping hot, stirring occasionally.

Meanwhile, combine the tomatoes and chilli (if using) and keep to one side. Combine the onion and cucumber in a small bowl, season with a big pinch of flaked sea salt and black pepper, add the chopped coriander and vinegar and stir well.

Heat a splash of oil in a large frying pan over a medium heat. Crack in the egg(s) and fry while the beans are reheating. When the eggs are done and the beans are hot, pour the beans into a bowl or on to a plate and place the egg(s) on top. Add the tomatoes and then the cucumber salad to the plate.

Put the tortilla into the pan you cooked the eggs in to warm through on both sides (this will only take a few seconds). When the tortilla is warmed, fold it and place on the side, add a wedge of lime and top with the remaining coriander leaves. Season the whole plate with sea salt and black pepper and serve with hot sauce.

In a quesadilla with sweet potato and cavolo nero

A quesadilla is basically a Mexican-style cheese toastie and is brilliant for using up leftovers. You can stick all sorts of things in between two tortillas, just add cheese and heat. Swap cavolo nero for spinach or sweet potato for butternut squash and use a different cheese or even a mixture of cheeses. This is a very forgiving recipe!

Serves 2
—

olive oil
1 small sweet potato, finely diced
140g cavolo nero, shredded
500g Black Beans – Refried If You
    Like (see recipe, pages 58–9)
2 spring onions, finely sliced
4 soft tortillas
4 tbsp Cheddar cheese, grated
2 heaped tbsp soured cream
flaked sea salt and freshly ground
    black pepper

For the quick pickled onions
(makes 4 portions)
125ml apple cider vinegar
1 tbsp sugar
1½ tsp flaked sea salt
½ red onion, peeled and finely sliced

To make the quick pickled onions, whisk the vinegar, 250ml of water, the sugar and flaked sea salt in a small bowl until dissolved. Add the onions and leave at room temperature for 1 hour, then cover and place in the fridge until you are ready to serve. Drain the onions just before serving. These will keep in the fridge for up to 2 weeks. Use any leftovers on the tostadas overleaf.

Heat 1 tablespoon of oil in a large frying pan over a medium heat, add the sweet potato and fry for 6–8 minutes, or until browned on all sides, stirring frequently. Add the cavolo nero and cook for 1 minute. Add the beans and cook for 1–2 minutes until hot through. Remove from the heat and add the spring onions.

Scrape the mixture into a bowl and clean the frying pan. Return to the heat, add a splash of oil and lay a tortilla in the pan. Sprinkle with a quarter of the cheese and once melting, spread half the bean and sweet potato mixture on top then sprinkle with another quarter of the cheese. Lay a second tortilla on top so that you have tortilla, cheese, beans and sweet potato, cheese, then tortilla. Fry for a couple of minutes until the base is golden, then carefully flip over to cook the other side until golden too.

Slide on to a chopping board and cut into 4–6 triangles. Cover with foil while you cook the second quesadilla. Drain the pickled onions and pile onto 2 plates with a dollop of soured cream and the quesadillas. Season with sea salt and black pepper and serve.

To make this gluten-free, use corn tortillas and for a vegan version, replace the prawns with smoked tofu and omit the soured cream.

On spicy prawn tostadas

I've done these as little bite-size canapé tostadas, to hand round at a party, or you can serve 3 per person as a starter. You can, of course, make them on bigger bases. After you've cut the circles out, chop the cut-offs into bite-size pieces, bake or fry them and use as croutons in a salad or sprinkled on a soup.

Serves 4
—

2 x 25cm soft tortillas
olive oil
500g Black Beans – Refried If You
    Like (see recipe, pages 58–9)
12–24 cooked king prawns
3 tbsp soured cream
1 little gem lettuce,
    shredded widthways
50g red cabbage, very finely sliced
2 portions of Quick Pickled Onions
    (see recipe, page 65) or Middle
    Eastern pickled turnips
2 radishes, finely sliced
2 heaped tbsp tinned sweetcorn
½ red chilli, very finely sliced
3 heaped tbsp pickled jalapeño
    slices, drained
1 small bunch of coriander
    (approx. 20g), leaves picked
    and roughly chopped
½ punnet of cress

For the prawn dressing
2 tsp extra-virgin olive oil
1 tsp hot sauce (I like to use Frank's)
½ lime, juiced
2 tbsp finely chopped
    coriander leaves
½ tsp ground cumin
1 tsp runny honey
½ tsp sweet smoked paprika
flaked sea salt

Preheat the oven to 180°C/350°F/Gas mark 4. Cut six 8cm circles out of each tortilla wrap using a cutter or a knife and a jam-jar lid. Line a baking tray with foil and arrange the small tortilla discs in a single layer.

Use your finger to rub each disc with a little oil on both sides. Bake in the hot oven for 5 minutes until golden around the edges. Remember the tortillas will crisp more as they cool.

Reheat the beans in a small pan over a medium-low heat until piping hot, stirring occasionally. They should take the same amount of time to heat through as the tortilla will take to crisp up in the oven.

Mix the ingredients for the prawn dressing together in a bowl with a big pinch of flaked sea salt, add the prawns, mix well and keep to one side.

In a small bowl, loosen the soured cream with a splash of water. Start to compile your tostadas by spreading a small spoonful of the beans on the tortilla bases. Top with a pinch each of lettuce and cabbage, a dollop of soured cream and a dressed prawn or two. Finish with a little of each of the remaining toppings and serve immediately.

Mushroom, lentil and walnut ragù

recipe overleaf

Mushroom, lentil and walnut ragù

This is basically a vegan Bolognese-style sauce and can be used in all the ways a meaty sauce made using mince can be...in a lasagne, on top of spaghetti or in one of the following four dishes.

Start by placing the porcini in a large jug, pour over 1 litre of just-boiled water and leave to one side to soak for 30 minutes.

While the porcini are soaking, heat the oil in a large saucepan over a medium heat. Add the onion, garlic and a pinch of flaked sea salt and cook for 5 minutes until softened but not browned, stirring occasionally.

Add the carrot, smoked paprika and button mushrooms. Turn the heat down to low and continue to cook for 20 minutes, stirring occasionally.

Add the wine, turn the heat up to high and bring to the boil. Use a spoon or spatula to scrape up all the flavour from the bottom of the pan and stir well. Add the bay leaves, tinned tomatoes, passata, lentils, oregano and pul biber. Use a slotted spoon to scoop out the soaking porcini mushrooms, roughly chop and add to the pan. Pour in the porcini soaking water, add a generous pinch of flaked salt and black pepper and bring to the boil. Turn the heat down to low and cook for 30 minutes, stirring deeply and thoroughly every few minutes, making sure to scrape the bottom of the pan.

cont.

Makes 12 portions
(approx. 300g each)

—

40g dried porcini mushrooms
4 tbsp olive oil
1 onion, peeled and finely diced
6 garlic cloves, peeled and grated
    or finely chopped
1 large carrot, peeled and finely diced
2 tsp smoked paprika
400g button mushrooms, finely diced
125ml red wine
3 bay leaves
2 x 400g tins chopped tomatoes
1 x 680g jar passata
500g green lentils, rinsed
4 tsp dried oregano
2 tsp pul biber (mild Turkish
    chilli flakes)
150g walnuts, chopped
2 tsp vegetable bouillon powder
1 small bunch of basil (approx. 20g),
    leaves picked and roughly torn
flaked sea salt and freshly ground
    black pepper

Add the walnuts, bouillon powder and 500ml of boiling water. Stir through the torn basil leaves, cover and cook for 20 minutes, stirring frequently. Finally, taste, season if needed and remove the bay leaves.

To freeze
Divide the ragù evenly between 12 sealable containers or freezer bags and leave to cool completely at room temperature. Label each portion with the recipe name and the date made, then place in the freezer and use within 3 months. Defrost in the fridge (it will take approximately 8 hours to defrost), then gently reheat in a saucepan over a medium-low heat until piping hot.

To chill
The ragù will be fine for 3 days in the fridge. Keep it covered and when you are ready to reheat, gently simmer in a saucepan over a medium-low heat until piping hot.

With rigatoni, feta and basil

I first made the ragù and served it like this when I went up to Edinburgh and filled my mates' freezer with loads of food after their twins were born. I made 24 portions and they were eating it for weeks. Once there was room in the freezer (which we bought from a local charity, specifically for the #batchcookingfornewparents project), the spaces got filled with packages of breast milk! I used rigatoni as it's much easier than spaghetti to eat with one hand, when the other hand is holding a baby. This is so easy and quick but really, really delicious and nutritious.

Serves 6

—

500g rigatoni
4 portions of Mushroom, Lentil and Walnut Ragù (see recipe, pages 70–1)
1 small bunch of basil (approx. 20g), leaves picked
200g feta cheese
flaked sea salt and freshly ground black pepper

Cook the pasta according to packet instructions then drain, reserving a little of the cooking water.

While the pasta is cooking, gently reheat the ragù in a saucepan over a medium-low heat until piping hot, stirring occasionally.

When the pasta is cooked and drained, return the pasta to the pan, tip in the hot ragù and stir in the larger basil leaves, adding a little of the reserved pasta water to loosen if needed.

Divide between 6 bowls, crumble over the feta, add the smaller basil leaves to decorate and finish with plenty of black pepper.

As a chilli with wedges, soured cream and cheese

I realised I was a bit snobby about chilli and wedges – gross versions, microwaved and slopped out in pubs and student unions across the land, have given the combo a bad name. But, if done well, it's a banging dish and cheap as chips. The chilli contains so much protein (lentils, kidney beans and walnuts) plus you're getting calcium and even more protein from the dairy on top. The dish is also full of fibre. This all equals an incredibly satisfying, filling dinner. Make sweet potato wedges instead or serve with a jacket potato, or tortillas, char-marked in the grill pan. All work brilliantly.

Serves 4
—

For the wedges
2 big or 4 small waxy potatoes
2 tsp olive oil
½ tsp smoked paprika
1 tsp dried oregano
flaked sea salt and freshly ground
    black pepper

For the chilli
1 tsp olive oil
1 tsp each of smoked paprika,
    cayenne pepper and ground cumin
½ tbsp ground coriander
½ tsp ground cinnamon
1 tbsp tomato purée
3 portions of Mushroom,
    Lentil and Walnut Ragù
    (see recipe, pages 70–1)
1 x 400g tin kidney beans, drained
    and rinsed (240g drained weight)
2 tbsp barbecue sauce

To serve
4 tbsp soured cream or
    Greek-style yoghurt
3 tbsp chopped coriander leaves
1 lime, quartered
80g Cheddar cheese, grated
2 tbsp pickled jalapeño slices or
    1 fresh red chilli, finely sliced

Preheat the oven to 200°C/400°F/Gas mark 6 and place a baking tray inside to heat up.

Start by making the wedges. Cut the potatoes in half lengthways, then cut each half into 4 or 5 wedges. Put them in a freezer bag with the oil, paprika, oregano, sea salt and black pepper, then seal the bag, shake, massage and jiggle the wedges around until well coated.

Carefully take the hot tray out of the oven, space out the wedges, skin-side down and cook for 25–35 minutes until golden brown and cooked through.

While the wedges are cooking, make the chilli. Heat the oil in a large saucepan over a low heat, add the spices and tomato purée and cook for 1 minute, stirring often. Add the ragù, kidney beans, barbecue sauce and a mugful of water. Stir well, bring to the boil, then turn the heat down to low and cook until piping hot throughout.

Serve the chilli with the wedges, a dollop of soured cream or yoghurt, the coriander, a wedge of lime and a sprinkling of cheese and chillies.

As a veggie shepherd's pie with a sweet potato, miso and smoked garlic mash

While being undoubtedly delicious, mashed sweet potato on its own can be very, well, sweet. Here, I've added smoked garlic and miso, along with smoked paprika and plenty of seasoning to balance out the sweetness with some serious notes of umami. I'm lucky enough to have some amazing greengrocers nearby in Bristol and I can buy smoked garlic from one of them. If you can't find it locally or at a farmer's market, it is also available to buy online, just search for (you guessed it) 'smoked garlic'. You can make this in individual ovenproof dishes (disposable foil dishes are great for this) and freeze them, ready to defrost and stick in the oven at a later date.

Serves 6

—

4–6 portions of Mushroom, Lentil and Walnut Ragù (see recipe, pages 70–1), depending on how hungry you are
buttered peas, to serve (optional)

For the mash
2–3 sweet potatoes, peeled and diced
45g salted butter
6 smoked garlic cloves, peeled and crushed
45g white miso paste
1 tsp smoked paprika
2 free-range egg yolks
flaked sea salt and freshly ground black pepper

Preheat the oven to 180°C/350°F/Gas mark 4.

Start by cooking the sweet potato, either by steaming over a pan of boiling water for 10–15 minutes until tender, or boiling in a pan of water over a medium-high heat for 10–15 minutes. Once cooked, drain and tip back into the pan. Add the rest of the mash ingredients, apart from the egg yolks, and mash together. Then stir until very well combined. Taste and adjust the seasoning, then add the egg yolks and stir well again.

Gently reheat the ragù in a saucepan over a medium-low heat until slightly warmed, but not piping hot, stirring occasionally. Pour the ragù into a baking dish approximately 20 x 30cm.

Pipe or spoon the mash on top of the ragù, starting at the edges and working towards the centre to avoid pushing the filling over the sides of the dish. Bake in the hot oven for approximately 35–40 minutes until golden brown and piping hot throughout. Serve with buttered peas.

With polenta, garlic spinach and Parmesan and rosemary crisps

Instant polenta, spinach that wilts and cooks as soon as you even show it the pan and Parmesan crisps that will be ready before you can say 'quick but impressive dinner'. This really is a winning dish. Smart enough for guests but simple enough if you're just making yourself a quick dinner before *EastEnders* starts. The Parmesan crisps make a really good nibble too.

Serves 4
—

3–4 portions of Mushroom, Lentil and Walnut Ragù (see recipe, pages 70–1), depending on your hunger levels

For the Parmesan crisps
8 heaped tsp finely grated Parmesan cheese
2 tsp finely chopped rosemary

For the spinach
2 tbsp salted butter
1–2 garlic cloves, peeled and crushed or grated
200g baby spinach
½ lemon

For the polenta
150g instant polenta
flaked sea salt

Preheat the oven to 200°C/400°F/Gas mark 6.

Start by making the Parmesan crisps. They need your full attention, but only for a few minutes.

Line a baking tray with non-stick greaseproof paper and then, using a teaspoon, make 8 small piles of grated Parmesan on the tray, spacing them out evenly. Sprinkle each pile with the rosemary. Flatten the mounds with your finger and pat down to form neat little circles, approximately 4cm in diameter. Put them in the oven and watch them like a *hawk*. They will burn very easily. You want to whip them out after about 4 minutes, when the cheese has melted and they have started to brown. They won't be crispy; this only happens once they come out of the oven. Leave to set for a minute, then use a palette knife to loosen them from the paper and let them cool while you get on with everything else.

Gently reheat the ragù in a saucepan over a medium-low heat until piping hot, stirring occasionally.

To cook the spinach, put the butter into a large frying pan or wok and sit the garlic on top of it. Place over a medium heat and let everything melt together. As soon as the butter has melted and the garlic is smelling fragrant, add half the spinach, stir to wilt down, then add the other half. Stir together, then cover with a lid and turn off the heat and allow to wilt while the polenta cooks.

cont.

To cook the polenta, pour 1 litre of boiling water into a medium saucepan, bring to the boil and add 1 tsp of flaked sea salt. Pour the polenta into the boiling water in a steady stream, whisking continuously with a balloon whisk. It should only take about 3 minutes to cook, but follow the instructions on the packet to be sure. Remove from the heat as soon as it can be described as 'smooth and consistent'. (The ideal partner?)

Divide the hot polenta between 4 bowls and top with the ragù. Use tongs to serve the spinach, leaving behind any liquid in the pan. Divide the spinach equally between the bowls. Add 2 Parmesan crisps to each bowl and squeeze a little lemon juice over the spinach before serving.

Building

Learn these techniques and you're opening up a whole world of new dishes

Blocks

Having an arsenal of goodies in your fridge and storecupboard is what takes your cooking to another level.

Whether it's a delicious sauce, some roasted veg or a piece of cooked fish, when you have something versatile and ready to eat, dinner can be on the table quickly and easily. The recipes in this chapter are the starting points – the building blocks. They are designed to inspire and structure your cooking.

These recipes cannot be frozen but they are incredibly versatile. You'll find nine base recipes, each with three completely different ways of serving them. These are only the start for you. They are designed to teach you new skills and increase your cooking 'vocabulary'. Nine delicious hero recipes that I hope will get used over and over again.

Once you've made the base and tried my suggestions, I'd love to see how else you use these ideas. Send me a pic on Twitter @pearcafe or Instagram @ellypear.

10-minute flatbreads

recipe overleaf

10-minute flatbreads

I first created this recipe for my last book but after the book had been printed, I started to discover more and more things I could do with it. So I'm delighted I've now got an opportunity to share some of them with you! The base recipe is ready in 10 minutes from the moment you decide to make the flatbreads until the moment they're on your plate; you don't need any special ingredients and, as you'll see, there's lots of things you can do with the dough as well as eat the breads as they are. These were a smash hit from *Fast Days & Feast Days* and I hope you can see why!

—

175g plain flour
flaked sea salt
olive oil

Put the flour, 100ml of cold water and a big pinch of flaked sea salt into a large bowl. Mix until the dough is just binding together but not too wet.

Dust a clean work surface with flour and knead the dough for 3 minutes. Roll it into a log and cut into 4 equal pieces then, with a floured rolling pin, roll out each piece of dough until approximately 15cm in diameter.

Pour just enough olive oil into the base of a large frying pan to coat the bottom and place over a medium-high heat.

One at a time, fry the flatbreads for 1 minute until the edges have hardened and the surface starts to bubble, then flip over and cook the other side for another minute or so until bubbly and golden brown.

Slide onto a plate and sprinkle with flaked sea salt. Cover loosely with a clean tea towel while you cook the others, serve immediately.

Topped with beetroot hummous, brown shrimps, nutmeg, dill and yoghurt

I was invited to do a demo at River Cottage and decided to make my 10-minute flatbreads and serve them with various toppings to showcase their versatility. When I arrived, my mate Gill Meller (long-time River Cottage head chef) showed me around the gardens and let me* pick a few things from the beds. I made the following combo up and topped them with nasturtium leaves and calendula petals too. Wholly optional, but very pretty. (*looked away while I…)

To make the hummous, chuck everything in a food processor with 1 teaspoon of flaked sea salt and a little black pepper and blitz until totally smooth. Taste for seasoning, then adjust with extra lemon juice, oil or tahini as necessary.

Make the flatbreads according to the recipe on pages 84–5. When they are cooked, smear each one with a couple of spoonfuls of beetroot hummous (leftover hummous keeps fine in the fridge for 3 days), sprinkle with the shrimps, then splatter with the yoghurt. Tear over the dill and grate over plenty of nutmeg before serving. These are great as a light lunch with a crisp green salad.

Serves 4

—

4 x 10-minute Flatbreads (see recipe, pages 84–5)
1 x 90g pack of brown shrimps
4 heaped tsp Greek-style yoghurt
a few sprigs of dill
1 whole nutmeg
crisp green salad, to serve

For the beetroot hummous
250g vac-packed cooked beetroot
1 x 400g tin chickpeas, drained and rinsed (240g drained weight)
2 tbsp extra-virgin olive oil
1 garlic clove, peeled and crushed
2 tbsp tahini
1 tbsp freshly squeezed lemon juice
flaked sea salt and freshly ground black pepper

Stuffed with halloumi

Halloumi is the perfect cheese to use for this as it stays pretty solid when you cook the flatbreads, and I like the little distinctive pieces poking through the surface. Why not try using the same technique to sandwich other things inside the bread before cooking? Some semi-dried tomatoes, roughly chopped and mixed with olives, work really well too.

Makes 4
—

4 x 10-minute Flatbreads (see recipe, pages 84–5)
100g halloumi cheese, finely diced
flaked sea salt
pul biber (mild Turkish chilli flakes)

Make the flatbreads up to the stage that the raw dough is rolled out. Put 25g of the diced halloumi on the surface of each one, leaving a 2cm border around the edge. Gather the edges into the centre so the whole thing looks like a little money pouch, then pinch together to seal and flip over. Gently flatten the parcel with your palm so it is round again then, with a floured rolling pin, roll it out until it is approximately 11cm in diameter.

Now the halloumi is sandwiched in the middle of the dough, fry as you would the plain breads on page 85. Sprinkle with flaked sea salt and pul biber and serve hot.

Smeared with roasted garlic butter and rosemary

Using this technique to roast a whole bulb of garlic will result in incredibly sweet, almost caramelised cloves that turn into a soft purée that you squeeze out of the papery casings. So satisfying! You could, of course, make this garlic butter and use it for something else (if you eat meat, why not smear it all over a chicken before roasting?). It freezes well too: just shape into a roll, wrap well in cling film and freeze. I love these with pasta for a delicious double carb hit.

Makes 4

—

1 garlic bulb
½ tsp olive oil
25g salted butter, softened
4 x 10-minute Flatbreads
   (see recipe, pages 84–5)
2 sprigs of rosemary, leaves
   finely chopped
flaked sea salt

Preheat the oven to 180°C/350°F/Gas mark 4. Slice off the top of the bulb of garlic, sit it on a square of foil, drizzle with the oil and wrap in the foil. Bake in the hot oven for 45 minutes, then remove and leave to cool. Once cooled, squeeze the garlic cloves into a bowl, discarding the skins. Add the butter and blend and grind with a spoon until smooth and uniform.

Cook the flatbreads as per the method on page 85. Spread with the butter, sprinkle with the rosemary and a pinch of flaked sea salt and serve immediately.

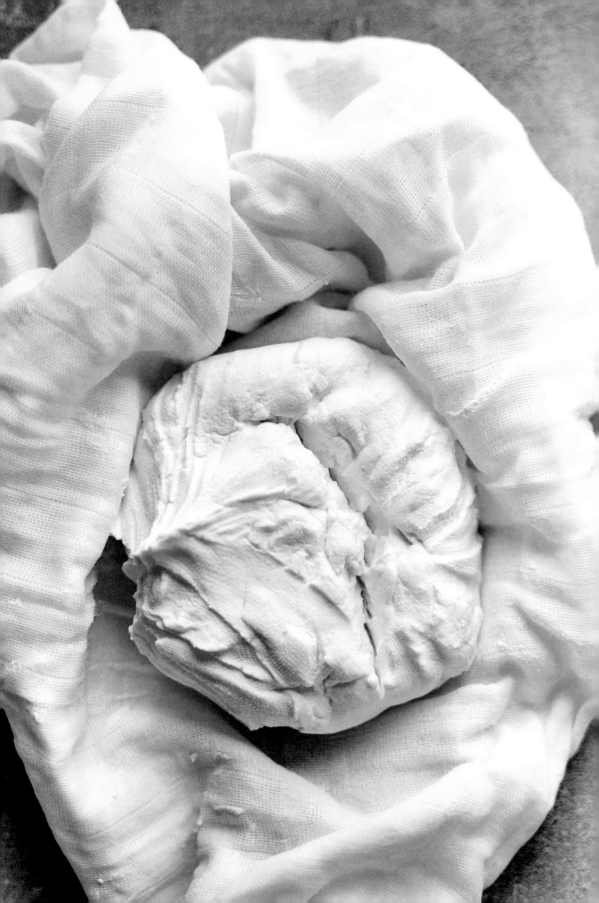

<u>Labneh</u>

With roasted beetroot, preserved lemon
gremolata and za'atar   94

Mixed with orange blossom water, served on
toast with toasted hazelnuts and honey   96

With chickpeas, courgettes and nigella seeds   99

recipe overleaf

Labneh

Labneh is simply strained yoghurt. I know this might not sound like the most interesting thing but, I promise you, once you learn how easy this is to do, you'll be using labneh in everything. The end product is a cross between Greek-style yoghurt and cream cheese, in both consistency and flavour. I bought a synthetic net strainer designed for straining jam from a local cookware shop for less than a fiver, but you can also use either a clean, new J-cloth or a piece of close-weave cotton muslin to make this.

—

1 heaped tsp flaked sea salt
1 x 500g tub plain, full-fat
   Greek-style yoghurt

Sit a sieve over a large bowl and lay over your chosen straining material. Simply stir the salt into the yoghurt (I tip the salt into the yoghurt pot and use a knife to mix well), then tip the whole lot into the lined sieve. The liquid dripping out should be pretty much clear – if white yoghurt is dripping out, your straining material is not fine enough. Tip the yoghurt back into the pot, double or triple over the material and start again.

Pull the edges of the material together and tie in a knot, then leave to drain. If your kitchen is hot, put the whole thing in the fridge to drain; otherwise a cool spot is fine (overnight in your kitchen, without the heating on, for example).

The sieve and bowl method is practical but for lots of people, hanging the labneh from the handle of a kitchen cabinet over a bowl or from the kitchen sink taps provides the perfect spot.

The longer you leave the yoghurt to drain, the thicker the labneh will be. I like it pretty thick and find that a good-quality, thick Greek-style yoghurt will take about 20–24 hours to reach the perfect consistency.

To store
Once drained, untie the material, tip the strained yoghurt into a sealable container and keep covered in the fridge for up to 3 days.

With roasted beetroot, preserved lemon gremolata and za'atar

This combo really shows off the labneh as the great neutral background for some punchy flavours. I've used beetroots with their leaves still attached, then used the leaves to make the gremolata, instead of the traditional parsley. I only discovered this works so well because I was recipe-testing in my PJs and I didn't have any parsley. I looked at the leaves I'd just trimmed off the beetroots and thought I'd use them instead. I'd cooked the leaves before but not tried using them raw. Lo and behold, it worked really well and along with the preserved lemons makes a delicious gremolata. I'd serve this as a starter but any leftovers can be mixed up to make a great packed lunch with the addition of some cooked rice or freekeh.

Serves 2 as a starter

—

3 small raw beetroot, leaves attached
1 tbsp olive oil
2 heaped tbsp Labneh (see recipe, pages 92–3)
2 tsp extra-virgin olive oil
flaked sea salt

For the gremolata
2 tbsp finely chopped preserved lemon rind
1–2 garlic cloves (depending on your taste), peeled and very finely chopped
2 tbsp finely chopped beetroot leaves (or substitute parsley leaves)

For the za'atar (makes a small jar that lasts forever – see page 143)
3 tbsp sesame seeds
2 tbsp dried thyme
3 tbsp ground sumac
1 tbsp flaked sea salt
1 tbsp ground cumin

Preheat the oven to 200°C/400°F/Gas mark 6 and trim the leaves off the beetroot, leaving about 2cm of the stalks intact. Wash and dry the beetroot, being careful not to tear the skins. Place in a roasting tin, pour over the olive oil and massage all over the beetroots before sprinkling with a pinch of flaked sea salt. Roast in the hot oven for 40–45 minutes until tender (a knife inserted should go through easily). Remove from the oven and leave to cool, then rub the skin off with your hands (it should come off easily).

To make the gremolata, mix all the ingredients together. For the za'atar, toast the sesame seeds in a dry pan over a medium heat for 1 minute until golden, shaking the pan often, then remove from the heat and mix with the remaining ingredients.

Divide the labneh between 2 plates and smear into a puddle. Cut the beetroot in half and put 3 halves on each plate. Sprinkle with the gremolata, 1 teaspoon of za'atar and drizzle with the extra-virgin olive oil to finish.

Mixed with orange blossom water, served on toast with toasted hazelnuts and honey

Labneh is great in so many dishes and can fit into breakfast, lunch and dinner plans. This is a great way to flavour it delicately and makes a really simple but special breakfast. I serve it with toasted seeded sourdough but I think it would also be delicious with toasted banana bread or Bread pudding too (see pages 102–3). You can get orange blossom water in Middle Eastern shops or online (souschef.co.uk and ocado.com both stock it). The vanilla salt was a delicious find from Halen Môn salt (and is available from them online) but I think you could replicate it pretty successfully with a little pinch of flaked sea salt with a teeny bit of vanilla mixed in.

Serves 1
—

70g Labneh (see recipe, pages 92–3)
1 tsp orange blossom water
10g hazelnuts
2 slices of seeded sourdough bread
1 tsp runny honey
1 pinch of vanilla salt

Combine the labneh with the orange blossom water and put to one side. Toast the hazelnuts in a dry pan over a medium heat for 1–2 minutes until golden brown, shaking the pan often, then remove from the heat and roughly chop. Toast the bread.

Spread the labneh on the toast, drizzle with the honey and sprinkle with the hazelnuts and vanilla salt.

Orange blossom water makes a great toner for sensitive or oily skin, or you can add it to your bath water for a luxurious fragrant soak.

Use up your leftovers

With chickpeas, courgettes and nigella seeds

This is a great salad that can be served warm or cold; it also scales up or down easily, so it's a great one for the mega courgette glut many gardeners experience in the summer. You could swap the chickpeas for cannellini or butter beans or even cooked Puy lentils. In winter, try the same with carrots instead of courgettes. You'd need to briefly boil them before frying, or try roasting them instead.

Serves 2 as a light lunch
—

2 tbsp extra-virgin olive oil
2 tbsp freshly squeezed lemon juice
1½ tsp ground cumin
2 courgettes (green and yellow, if possible)
1 garlic clove, peeled and crushed or grated
2 tbsp chopped flat-leaf parsley leaves
240g home-cooked dried chickpeas or 1 x 400g tin chickpeas, drained and rinsed (240g drained weight)
3 tbsp Labneh (see recipe, pages 92–3)
½ tsp nigella seeds
flaked sea salt and freshly ground black pepper

Combine the olive oil, lemon juice, cumin and a good pinch of black pepper in a bowl and whisk. Cut the courgettes into 1cm-thick diagonal slices, add to the bowl and mix well.

Place a large frying pan over a high heat until very hot. Use tongs to remove the courgette slices from the marinade and fry in batches until browned on both sides.

Add the garlic and parsley to the marinade and mix well, then add the chickpeas and the cooked courgettes and toss everything together. Divide between two bowls or plates and dot with the labneh. Sprinkle with the nigella seeds, season with flaked sea salt and serve.

Bread pudding

recipe overleaf

Bread pudding

First of all, I feel compelled to point out that bread pudding is not the same as bread and butter pudding. Bread pudding is far simpler to make, cheaper, quicker and much more versatile.

Do you want to make a cake? Do you want to make it with storecupboard ingredients (or things that you'll definitely be able to find in your local corner shop)? Do you want to chuck it all together in a slightly haphazard way and not worry too much about things not being spot on? Do you want a forgiving recipe that you can't really screw up? Well then, this is the cake for you. A recipe handed down through the generations of my mate Dan's family. An East End classic. I've swapped the water the bread is usually soaked in for tea, 'cause I'm swanky like that. Use whatever bread you need to use up (a bit more or less than 375g is fine, but I'd avoid using seeded bread) and use whatever sugar you like. This is a cool, chilled recipe. Pretty much anything goes.

—

2 tea bags
375g bread (stale is best)
125g sultanas
100g self-raising flour
4 tbsp marmalade
50g caster sugar
65g light soft brown sugar
90g salted butter, cubed,
    plus extra for greasing
3 free-range eggs, beaten
2 heaped tbsp mixed spice

Preheat the oven to 180°C/350°F/Gas mark 4.

Brew the tea bags in 1.2 litres of boiling water. Rip the bread into whole walnut-sized pieces and combine with the sultanas in a large bowl. Pour over half the tea and leave to one side until it has absorbed, then pour over the rest and leave to soak for about half an hour. Once soaked, tip the mixture into a colander and squeeze out the excess liquid. Return to the bowl and add the flour, marmalade, sugars, 50g of the butter, eggs and mixed spice.

Grease two 23 x 13cm loaf tins, divide the mixture between the tins and dot another 20g of butter on the top of each loaf.

Cover with foil and bake in the hot oven for 1 hour 45 minutes, then remove the foil and bake for another 15 minutes.

To store
The loaves will keep well wrapped in foil, at room temperature for about 3 or 4 days. You can also slice the loaves and freeze them in freezer bags, to be defrosted at room temperature at a future date.

Fried in butter with cherries and crème fraîche

After you've enjoyed a slice or two of the bread pudding, this is another way of serving it that you could use as a pudding or for a really delicious weekend brunch. A hot, fried, crispy slice of bread pudding, topped with the cool, sharp crème fraîche and a few cherries, makes a great combo. The chocolate adds a Black Forest gâteau feel to the dish...

Serves 2

—

20g salted butter
2 slices of Bread Pudding
   (see recipe, pages 102–3)
2 tbsp crème fraîche
50g cherries
dark chocolate, finely grated
   (optional)

Heat a large frying pan over a medium heat and, when hot, add the butter. Place the slices of bread pudding in the pan and fry on both sides until golden. This should take about 4–5 minutes.

Place the slices on 2 small plates and add the crème fraîche, top with cherries and sprinkle over the grated chocolate (if using).

Hot with vanilla custard

Serves 2, generously

—

2 slices of Bread Pudding
    (see recipe, pages 102–3)

For the custard (makes
approx. 300ml)
2 free-range eggs
50g caster sugar
½ tsp cornflour
150ml double cream
150ml whole milk
½ vanilla pod

There are so many ways to vary the classic custard recipe – use cream or milk or a combination of the two, more or less eggy, more or less sweet. This, here, is exactly how I like it. Heavily speckled with vanilla seeds and not too sweet. A little cornflour to thicken it and made using the very best-quality eggs with really orange yolks for a vivid yellow custard.

Separate the eggs, put the yolks in a large bowl (keep the whites for something else) add the sugar to the egg yolks then whisk with a balloon whisk for about 30 seconds until pale and thick. Add the cornflour and whisk again.

Pour the cream and milk into a saucepan. Scrape out the seeds from the vanilla pod half, then add both the seeds and pod to the pan. Place over a medium-low heat until almost boiling, then remove from the heat, discard the vanilla pod and very slowly pour the hot liquid on to the eggs and sugar, whisking continuously.

Pour the mixture back into the pan, place over a very low heat and stir the custard continuously until thickened. This can take up to 10 minutes, so do not rush it. You don't want scrambled eggs! The custard can be served straight away or reheated gently when needed. Serve with the Bread pudding (it's really good warmed up in the oven while you make your custard).

Bread pudding

With apple compote and cinnamon sugar

A cold slice of Bread pudding, topped with warm apple compote and sprinkled with cinnamon sugar, makes a great afternoon snack or pudding. The compote is also lovely on top of a bowl of yoghurt and granola for breakfast. My great-grandma Cissie always had a bowl of cooked apple in the fridge, with a plate on top. If you use eating apples (I like to use Granny Smiths) rather than cooking apples, you probably won't need to add any sugar.

Serves 2, generously
—

2 slices of Bread Pudding
    (see recipe, pages 102–3)

For the cinnamon sugar
50g caster sugar
1 tbsp ground cinnamon

For the compote
½ lemon, juiced
4 Granny Smith apples
2 tsp soft brown sugar (optional)

To make the cinnamon sugar, simply pour the sugar and cinnamon into a small jar and shake well. This will keep forever and can be used on loads of things. Just keep the jar sealed and store in a cool, dry place.

Fill a bowl with cold water and add the lemon juice. Peel only 2 of the apples. Core all 4 apples and chop into 1–2cm dice (I like the rustic effect of having some apples peeled and some unpeeled in various-sized cubes, but if you prefer a more uniform, smooth compote-style apple purée, peel all the apples and cut into 1.5cm dice). Add the apples to the water and use both hands to scoop up the chunks and put them into a medium saucepan. Keep the lemony water. Place the pan over a medium heat and cook until the apple starts to break down, adding a couple of spoonfuls of the lemony water if it's drying out.

After a few minutes, turn the heat right down and cover. Stir regularly and, again, add a little more lemony water if it's looking dry. After about 20 minutes, the apple will be almost completely broken down, with a few chunks. Taste and if you'd like it sweeter, add a little brown sugar. Serve with the Bread pudding and sprinkle with cinnamon sugar. Any leftover compote can be eaten hot or cold and will keep fine covered in the fridge for a couple of days.

Marinated peppers

recipe overleaf

Marinated peppers

These strips of red pepper in a herby marinade are such a great staple to have in the fridge. Use them in salads, sandwiches, with scrambled eggs or in one of the recipes on the following pages. Just adjust the herbs according to what you find and your own personal taste.

Makes approx. 300g (drained weight)
—

4 tbsp olive oil, plus extra
6 red peppers
1 tbsp red wine vinegar
1 tbsp capers, drained
2 tbsp oregano leaves
2 tbsp finely chopped flat-leaf parsley
a few small basil leaves
1 garlic clove, peeled and finely grated
pinch of sugar
flaked sea salt and freshly
    ground black pepper

Put a little oil in the palm of your hand and one by one, rub the surface of the peppers with oil. Put them on a baking tray under a hot grill, turning occasionally until the skin is blackened all over – this will take about 30 minutes. While they cook, make the dressing.

Combine 4 tablespoons of olive oil with the vinegar, capers, oregano, flat-leaf parsley, basil and garlic in a bowl and whisk. Season with flaked sea salt, black pepper and a pinch of sugar. Taste and adjust the vinegar if necessary.

When the peppers are blackened all over, put in a large bowl, cover with cling film and leave to one side to steam for 2–3 minutes. Then peel off the skins, halve, remove the stalks, deseed and slice into 1cm strips.

Tip into 2 large lidded glass jars or a sealable container and pour over the dressing to cover, topping up with oil if needed so that the peppers are fully submerged. Seal with a lid.

To store
Place in the fridge, where they will sit happily for at least 3 or 4 days.

In a frittata with ricotta and spinach

A green, red and white frittata – an edible Italian flag. Mix the spinach into the body of the frittata but keep the peppers and ricotta on the surface to show them off. It keeps really well wrapped in the fridge and makes a great packed lunch. We are famous for our frittata at The Pear Café and make loads of combinations, although the base is always potato, Cheddar and egg. Look up #pearcafefrittata on Instagram for hundreds of ideas.

Serves 8
—

12 new potatoes, scrubbed
1 tbsp salted butter
olive oil
2 large handfuls of spinach
6 free-range eggs
250g mature Cheddar cheese, grated
100g Marinated Peppers, drained
    (see recipe, pages 110–11)
60g ricotta
flaked sea salt and freshly ground
    black pepper

Put the potatoes into a medium saucepan. Cover with cold water, add a pinch of salt and bring to the boil over a high heat. Turn the heat down to medium, cover and simmer for 15 minutes until tender, then drain and leave to cool. Once cooled, slice into thick discs.

Heat the butter and 1 tablespoon of oil in a 25cm non-stick frying pan over a medium heat. Fry the potatoes for 10–15 minutes until golden brown on both sides. Use a slotted spatula to transfer to a plate to cool. Return the pan to the heat, add the spinach to the residual oil/butter and cook briefly until wilted, stirring, then add to the potatoes. Crack the eggs into a jug and whisk. Season well, then stir in the Cheddar, fried potatoes and spinach.

Preheat the grill. Thoroughly wipe out the frying pan, then place it over a medium heat. Add a little olive oil and once hot, pour in the egg mixture. Using a heatproof rubber spatula, drag the edges towards the centre, tipping the pan and letting the liquid egg flow into the gaps. This helps the entire mixture to set, not just the bottom. Continue for 5 minutes until almost set. Spread the peppers over the frittata and dot the ricotta in between. Place the pan under the grill (keep the handle out if it is plastic) and grill until golden.

cont.

Remove and leave to cool in the pan for 5 minutes. Gently slide the frittata onto a chopping board and leave to cool for a further 5 minutes. Slice into 8 and serve.

In linguine with anchovies

Serves 4

—

500g linguine
1 tbsp olive oil (you can use the
    oil from the marinated peppers,
    if you like)
6 anchovy fillets
200g Marinated Peppers, drained
    (see recipe, pages 110–11)
1 small handful of black olives,
    stoned and sliced (optional)
1 small handful of basil leaves
flaked sea salt and freshly
    ground black pepper
Parmesan cheese, finely grated,
    to serve
a few basil leaves, to serve
4 tsp extra-virgin olive oil, to serve
green salad, to serve

If you've got the jar of peppers in the fridge, the sauce will be ready in less time than the pasta takes. A great midweek dinner that will be on the table in less than 15 minutes.

Cook the pasta according to packet instructions, then drain and reserve a little of the cooking water.

While the pasta is cooking, heat the oil in a large frying pan over a medium heat, add the anchovies and stir until the anchovy fillets have melted into the oil. Add the peppers and olives (if using), and cook for a minute or so until the peppers have warmed though.

When the pasta is cooked and drained, tip the linguine into the frying pan, add the basil leaves and add a little of the reserved pasta water to loosen, if needed.

Season well with black pepper and use a pair of tongs to mix it all together.

Divide between 4 bowls, sprinkle with grated Parmesan, garnish with a few basil leaves and drizzle with a little of your best extra-virgin olive oil before serving with a green salad.

A simple mixture of 4 anchovy fillets, finely chopped and blended with a tablespoon of salted butter, is great with seared scallops and asparagus. Just fry the scallops (see page 194) and a handful of asparagus spears (halved lengthways) in a little oil. Once browned on both sides, add the anchovy butter and a squeeze of lemon juice to the pan. Sprinkle over finely chopped parsley or tarragon and serve.

With burrata, asparagus and toast

Burrata is an incredible cheese — very much like mozzarella but the core is basically double cream. It's as delicious as that suggests. One ball is great between 4 people as a starter or as part of an antipasti spread. Put everything in the middle of the table and let your guests build their own bruschetta by piling a spoonful of cheese on to a piece of toast, then topping with some of the peppers and some asparagus pieces. A bowl of good-quality, homemade pesto on the side makes a nice addition too.

Serves 4

—

8 asparagus spears
4–8 slices of sourdough bread
extra-virgin olive oil
1 x 200g ball of burrata
a few small basil leaves
200g Marinated Peppers, drained (see recipe, pages 110–11)
flaked sea salt and freshly ground black pepper

Trim the asparagus and bring a pan of salted water to the boil over a medium-high heat. Carefully drop the asparagus into the boiling water, bring back to the boil and cook for 2 minutes or a little longer for thick stalks. Drain the boiling water, then cool the asparagus under cold running water to stop it from cooking and to keep its bright green colour. Cut diagonally into bite-size pieces.

Drizzle the bread with olive oil on both sides and griddle until toasted. Put the burrata into a small serving bowl, drizzle more olive oil over the surface, season with flaked sea salt and black pepper and top with the basil leaves.

Arrange the toast, burrata, asparagus and peppers on a board. Take to the table and let guests build their own bruschetta.

Satay dressing

recipe overleaf

Satay dressing

The only problem with making this peanut sauce is you'll end up wanting to down it straight from the jar. It's addictive stuff. It makes a great dipping sauce and salad dressing and is also great on Buddha bowls and lots of noodle dishes.

Makes 6 portions
—

1 tsp light soft brown sugar
2 tsp freshly squeezed lime juice
4 tbsp peanut butter (smooth or chunky is fine, and I actually find the cheaper versions work best)
3 tbsp rice wine vinegar
1 tbsp soy sauce
1½ tbsp vegetable, sunflower or rapeseed oil
1½ tbsp Sriracha, to taste
2 tbsp sesame oil

Dissolve the sugar in the lime juice, then put it into a blender with all the remaining ingredients and blend until smooth. Taste and adjust as you see fit. That's it.

To store
Once made, it will keep fine in a jar in the fridge for ages.

Noodle salad

A huge crunchy salad packed full of veg that keeps really well. The lunchbox and picnic dream. The first time I made this, I lived off a huge batch for three days in a row. They were good times. Feel free to change the veg for whatever you fancy – just keep it crunchy and raw and include as many different varieties as possible.

Serves 4
—

1 corn on the cob or approx. 130g tinned sweetcorn
75g soba noodles, uncooked
sesame oil
2 tbsp peanuts
75g red cabbage, finely sliced
1 pepper (red, orange or yellow), deseeded and sliced
⅓ cucumber, halved lengthways, deseeded and sliced into ½cm thick half-moons
60g ripe cherry tomatoes, halved
75g Chinese cabbage, shredded
1 spring onion, finely sliced
1 small carrot, peeled and cut into fine matchsticks
75g fine green beans, trimmed
30g broccoli, finely chopped
4 tbsp roughly chopped coriander leaves
4 tbsp roughly chopped mint leaves
6 tbsp Satay Dressing (see recipe, page 120)
flaked sea salt and freshly ground black pepper
lime wedges, to serve

Image p. 125

If using a corn on the cob, cook in a pan of boiling water over a medium heat for 5 minutes until tender, then drain and leave to cool. Cook the noodles according to the packet instructions, then drain, rinse thoroughly in cold water, drain again, tip into a large bowl and toss in a little sesame oil to stop them sticking.

Meanwhile, toast the peanuts in a dry pan over a medium heat for 1–2 minutes until golden brown, shaking the pan often. Remove from the heat and roughly chop.

Once the corn has cooled, stand it on its end and carefully slice off the kernels with a sharp knife.

Tip all the vegetables and half the herbs in with the noodles and pour half the Satay dressing over the top. Toss everything together really well with very clean hands. Taste and season with flaked sea salt and black pepper.

Transfer the dressed noodles to 4 serving bowls and garnish with the peanuts, lime wedges and remaining chopped herbs. Put the other half of the dressing on the table so people can add more if they like.

Prawn summer rolls

Summer rolls are just like spring rolls but instead of being fried, you simply soak rice paper wrappers in water and fill them with lots of delicious things. The secret to success with these Vietnamese classics is to have everything ready before you start. You need to work quickly but carefully, as the wet rice paper wrappers are very delicate. You'll find these wrappers in Asian supermarkets, and many big supermarkets now stock them too. Prawns, veg and fine noodles is my favourite combo but you can lay out all sorts of prepped things and have fun sitting around the table with your mates making your own rolls. Give each person their own dish of satay sauce to avoid any double-dipping-related arguments.

Makes 12

—

50g dried thin rice noodles (vermicelli)
2 Chinese lettuce leaves
12 x 16cm rice paper wrappers
1 small bunch of mint (approx. 20g), leaves picked
1 small bunch of coriander (approx. 20g), leaves picked
165g cooked king prawns
4 tbsp roasted peanuts, finely chopped (optional)
½ carrot, peeled and cut into fine matchsticks
6 tbsp Satay Dressing (see recipe, page 120), to serve

Cook the noodles according to the packet instructions. Drain, refresh under cold water, drain again and set aside.

Lay the Chinese lettuce leaves on top of each other, then roll up and shred into very thin ribbons approximately 2mm wide.

Get a shallow bowl big enough to hold the rice paper and fill with warm water. Take one wrapper, submerge it in the water for 10 seconds, take it out really carefully and lay it on a plate. Lay a mint leaf and a couple of coriander leaves in the centre. Place two prawns on top of the herbs and sprinkle with the peanuts (if using). Add about 1 tablespoon of the noodles, a few pieces of carrot and a pinch of shredded Chinese leaf.

Take the edge nearest to you and roll it over the filling. Bring the two sides into the centre, then roll away from you into a tight parcel. Repeat until you have used all the wrappers. Serve with the dressing as a dip.

Five-spice smoked tofu nuggets

I've basically made vegan chicken nuggets by accident. Honestly. And I don't regret it for a minute. These things are ridiculously delicious and I can't recommend them enough. They're great on the end of skewers and dipped into the Satay sauce as party food. But if you don't want to serve this as a canapé, the cubes of tofu are delicious on a bed of brown rice with some pak choy and the Satay sauce drizzled over the top. The recipe would work well with pieces of chicken too, if you eat meat.

The tofu you choose is important. You want to look for one that comes as a big, solid, wet cube and nearly always in a cardboard box. Open the box and inside you'll see a block of tofu in a little liquid, sealed inside a plastic package. The recipe requires this soft, wet kind to create the steam inside the crust that makes it puff up.

Makes 8

—

1 x 225g box of smoked tofu (see my guide to tofu on page 19)
2 tbsp cornflour
½ tsp Chinese five-spice powder
a large pinch of smoked paprika
300ml vegetable oil
2–4 tbsp Satay Dressing (see recipe, page 120)
flaked sea salt

Lay the block of tofu on a few sheets of kitchen paper. Fold another sheet of kitchen paper and use to press down gently on the top to absorb the moisture.

Cut the tofu into 8 equal-sized cubes. Put the cornflour in a shallow bowl, add the five-spice powder and paprika and mix well. Toss the tofu cubes in the spiced cornflour until they are dusted on all sides.

Pour the vegetable oil into a wok and place over a high heat. Once hot, shake off any excess flour then very carefully lower each nugget into the hot oil using a slotted spoon or tongs. Deep-fry, turning regularly (and very carefully), for 4–5 minutes until all sides are golden brown and crisp. Remove the tofu from the pan using a slotted spoon or tongs and drain on kitchen paper. Sprinkle the cubes with flaked sea salt while they are still hot – this helps to keep them crispy. Thread them on to skewers and serve with the dressing for dipping.

Poached Salmon

recipe overleaf

Poached salmon

Poaching fish in an aromatic broth like this one is fast, easy and results in a delicate, soft texture. Delicious, but definitely in need of some contrast, which you can get by serving it alongside something pickled, crunchy, toasted or sharp. The same technique works with lots of fish but I prefer to use fatty fish like salmon and trout – poached white fish cooked in water like this can end up a bit insipid. You're better off poaching fish such as haddock in milk: follow the same directions opposite, but swap the lemon for white onion.

—

2 bay leaves
1 small bunch of flat-leaf
    parsley (approx. 20g)
5 peppercorns
½ lemon, sliced
½ small onion, peeled
2 salmon fillets (approx.
    140g each)
flaked sea salt

Put all the ingredients apart from the salmon in a wide-based saucepan (keep the bunch of parsley whole, stalks and all). Add ½ teaspoon of flaked sea salt and pour in 1 litre of water. Place over a high heat and bring to the boil, then reduce the heat to low, cover and simmer for 5 minutes.

Carefully lower the salmon fillets into the pan, cover and gently simmer for 7 minutes.

Remove and drain the fish using a slotted spatula, reserving the poaching liquid (see recipe, page 130). Peel away and discard the skin. Enjoy the poached salmon hot or cold.

To store
It will keep for 1–2 days covered in the fridge.

Flaked over giant couscous with tahini yoghurt and pickled cucumber

This recipe makes four starter-size portions and is plated up in quite a restaurant-style way, but there are lots of other ways you can serve this dish. Feel free to chuck it all into a sealable container box to make a great packed lunch, or even poach a whole side of salmon for a party and serve on a bed of the couscous and cucumber with the tahini yoghurt on the side.

Serves 4, as a starter

—

1 litre of salmon poaching liquid (see recipe, pages 128–9) or 1 fish stock cube or 3 tsp bouillon powder
100g giant couscous
3 tsp chermoula (available in jars from large supermarkets, or online)
100g Greek-style yoghurt
40g tahini
1 medium cucumber
2 tsp extra-virgin olive oil, plus extra for drizzling
2 tsp white wine vinegar
1 portion of Poached Salmon (see recipe, pages 128–9)
a few sprigs of dill
flaked sea salt and freshly ground black pepper

Chermoula is a deeply herbal and slightly spicy Moroccan sauce, bright with the flavours of lemon, coriander and parsley. If you can't find it (look for Belazu jars), you can substitute it with 2 tablespoons of extra-virgin olive oil and 1 teaspoon of freshly squeezed lemon juice blitzed with a few sprigs of coriander and a pinch each of cayenne pepper, ground cumin and paprika.

Place a saucepan over a high heat and pour in 1 litre of the salmon poaching liquid (see recipe, pages 128–9). If you don't have the poaching liquid reserved, dissolve 1 fish stock cube or 3 teaspoons of bouillon powder in 1 litre of boiling water and pour into the pan. Bring the stock or poaching water to the boil. Add the couscous, turn the heat down to medium-low and simmer for 7 minutes, stirring occasionally. Drain in a sieve and rinse with cold water to stop it cooking further. Tip the cooked couscous into a small bowl and add the chermoula. Stir well to combine and set to one side. Mix the yoghurt and tahini together in a small bowl. Season with sea salt and set to one side.

Using a vegetable peeler, peel the skin off the cucumber and discard, then peel wide ribbons from the cucumber, stopping when you get to the seedy core. Put the cucumber ribbons into a bowl, dress with the extra-virgin olive oil and the white wine vinegar and season with flaked sea salt and black pepper.

To plate up, mix the couscous with the cucumber ribbons. Spoon a puddle of tahini yoghurt onto 4 plates. Top with the couscous and cucumber mixture. Flake the salmon equally between the 4 plates. Drizzle each plate with a little of your best olive oil. Season with flaked sea salt and black pepper and decorate with a few sprigs of dill.

Chermoula can be used in so many ways. It can be brushed onto a halved aubergine before grilling. Meat eaters could mix some chermoula with yoghurt and use it to marinate a chicken before roasting. It also works really well smeared over a salmon fillet before baking. Try thinning it down with a little extra-virgin olive oil and use it to dress a salad.

Ways to use up chermoula

Poached salmon

With leeks, new potatoes and a mustard vinaigrette

Serves 2

—

250g new potatoes, scrubbed
2 leeks, trimmed and sliced into
    2cm slices, or 6 whole baby
    leeks, halved widthways
olive oil
1 heaped tbsp baby capers, drained
1 tbsp salted butter
1 portion of Poached Salmon (see
    recipe, pages 128–9)
flaked sea salt

For the dressing
1 tbsp Dijon mustard
1½ tbsp red wine vinegar
2 tbsp extra-virgin olive oil
flaked sea salt and freshly
    ground black pepper

A simple warm salad, smart enough to serve guests but equally happy packed into a lunchbox. What a guy.

Put the potatoes into a medium saucepan. Cover with cold water, add a pinch of salt and bring to the boil over a high heat. Turn the heat down to medium, cover and simmer for 15 minutes until tender. When the potatoes are cooked, remove them from the water and leave to cool. Put the leeks into the simmering water and cook for 4–6 minutes until tender, then drain. Once cooled, halve the potatoes, quartering any large ones.

Heat 1 tablespoon of olive oil in a large frying pan over a medium heat, add the capers and fry for a few seconds until crispy. Remove the capers from the pan and drain on kitchen paper.

Wipe out the pan and add another tablespoon of olive oil and the butter. Place over a medium heat, add the potatoes and fry for 5 minutes until golden, shaking the pan occasionally. Add the leeks and sauté everything together for another couple of minutes until the leeks are soft and golden brown. Turn the heat off and leave the veg in the pan while you make the dressing.

Put all the dressing ingredients into a large bowl, whisk thoroughly to combine, season well with flaked sea salt and black pepper, then taste and adjust the seasoning if necessary. Tip in the warm potatoes and leeks and, using a tablespoon, carefully but thoroughly fold to combine. Gently flake in the salmon and very carefully fold together, trying not to break the fish up too much.

Divide between 2 bowls and top with the crispy capers.

On toast with poached egg, greens and aïoli

This combo is inspired by one of my favourite Bristol brunch spots, Katie and Kim's Kitchen in Montpelier. Everything tastes incredible because they use great ingredients, cook brilliantly and put tonnes of butter in everything. Brunch heaven.

Serves 2

—

1 handful of greens of your choice – asparagus, spring greens or blanched tenderstem broccoli all work well
2 tsp salted butter, plus extra for the toast
1 tbsp white wine vinegar
2 very fresh free-range eggs
2 slices of good-quality bread
1 portion of Poached Salmon (see recipe, pages 128–9)
2 tbsp aïoli (see recipe, page 54) or hollandaise (optional)
flaked sea salt and freshly ground black pepper
a couple of sprigs of soft herbs such as dill or tarragon, to serve

Wash the greens and shake dry. Heat the butter in a frying pan over a high heat and sauté the greens (in other words, fry hot and fast) for 2–3 minutes until cooked. Remove the pan from the heat, cover with foil and set aside while you get on with the rest.

Three-quarters fill a medium saucepan with boiling water and add the vinegar. Place over a medium-high heat and crack the eggs into 2 separate cups.

Once the water is boiling, use a balloon whisk to whip the water into a whirlpool. Carefully and with confidence, lower the side of the cup containing the first egg as close to the water as possible and slip the egg right into the vortex. Immediately turn the heat down so that it's nearly off. If you're using an electric hob that stays hot long after you've turned it down, move the pan on to another ring over a very low heat – too vigorous a boil and your egg will burst. The vortex will whip the egg into a neat round. Leave it untouched for 2 minutes, until the white has set and the yolk is still runny. Using a slotted spoon, carefully lift the egg out of the water and on to a plate. Place a bowl upside down over it to keep it warm. Repeat to poach the second egg.

While the second egg is poaching, toast the bread. To serve, put a piece of toast on each plate, butter it liberally and lay the greens on top. Divide the salmon between the toasts, flaking it evenly, top with the poached egg, dress with a spoonful of aïoli or hollandaise, and garnish with the herbs. Season well with flaked sea salt and black pepper and serve.

Green harissa

recipe overleaf

Green harissa

This powerful, vibrant sauce is a great thing to have in the fridge. I was sent a big tub to try by Belazu and became so addicted to it I decided to try making my own. It has a particular affinity with eggs but I've found all sorts of other ways to use it too. Here's the base recipe and three of my favourite serving suggestions.

Makes 4 portions

—

1 small bunch of coriander (approx. 20g), stalks and leaves chopped
2 spring onions, roughly chopped
2 level tbsp sliced pickled jalapeños, drained
25g cavolo nero or kale, roughly chopped
1–2 garlic cloves, peeled and chopped
2 tbsp vegetable oil
extra-virgin olive oil
flaked sea salt

Put all the harissa ingredients apart from the olive oil into a food processor with a big pinch of flaked sea salt and whizz until it becomes a smooth paste. Tip into a jar and pour in enough olive oil to make sure that the harissa paste is fully submerged, then seal with a lid.

This is the same mixture, before you add the olive oil, that is used in the green rice on page 60.

To store
Keep in the fridge, where it will last for a week.

With freekeh, halloumi and cherries

Freekeh is an ancient type of grain that looks similar to brown rice but is actually a type of wheat that is harvested while young and green. The grains are toasted, then their outer layers are rubbed off, leaving just the inner core. Nutty, firm and chewy, it has a slightly smoky taste and a myriad of nutritional benefits. It is high in protein and fibre (higher than quinoa), which means it'll keep you feeling full. It's also low GI and high in iron, calcium and zinc. If you can't find it (big supermarkets stock it by the couscous), you can get it online. There's also a ready-to-eat kind available, which would make this recipe super-quick.

Serves 2

—

1 tbsp olive oil
1 small red onion, peeled and diced
140g freekeh
1 lemon, halved
1 x 200g packet of halloumi cheese, cut into 6 slices
2–3 tbsp Green Harissa (see recipe, pages 138–9)
a few cherries, destoned and quartered
½ tsp za'atar (see recipe, page 94)
flaked sea salt

Heat the olive oil in a saucepan over a low heat, add the diced onion and a pinch of flaked sea salt and cook for about 10 minutes, or until softened, stirring occasionally.

Add the freekeh, stir well and pour in 350ml of boiling water. Bring back to the boil, cover, reduce the heat to low and simmer for about 20 minutes until the water is almost all absorbed; the grains should still be al dente. Remove from the heat, drain in a sieve, tip back into the pan, cover and leave to one side to steam.

Preheat a griddle pan over a high heat so it's good and hot, then sear the lemon halves cut side-down. Griddle the halloumi slices for 2–3 minutes until golden brown, turning halfway through.

Tip the freekeh into a large bowl and add the green harissa. Mix well and divide between 2 plates or bowls. Tuck the halloumi slices into the piles of freekeh and put a lemon half on each plate. Top with with cherry halves and a sprinkling of za'atar.

Green eggs on rye – recipe overleaf

TIP

Put a little dish of za'atar on a board with a dish of olive oil or argan oil and some bread. Dip the bread in the oil, then in the za'atar. Devour with drinks.

More za'atar recipes on page 94, 140 and 180

Green eggs on rye

Spreading green harissa on toast and topping with a 6-minute egg is one of the simplest pleasures. I make this often and I've found an incredible dense seeded rye bread called Fjord from The Real Patisserie, a bakery in Brighton, that works brilliantly. The widely available (rectangular) dense rye bread with sunflower seeds is great too and easier to get hold of.

Serves 2

—

2 free-range eggs
4 slices of seeded dark rye or
   pumpernickel bread
2 tbsp Green Harissa (see recipe,
   pages 138–9)
flaked sea salt and freshly
   ground black pepper

Make sure the eggs are at room temperature. Fill a small saucepan with boiling water and bring to a continuous boil over a medium heat. Gently lower the eggs into the boiling water and immediately set your timer for 6 minutes.

While the eggs cook, toast the bread. When the timer goes off, pour away the hot water, holding your eggs back with a spoon. Sit the (now dry) pan in the sink and turn the cold tap on, blasting the eggs until totally cold. Roll the eggs on the counter, pressing down gently, until the shell cracks all over. Peel very carefully. Use a very sharp knife to cut them in half, lengthways.

Spread the Green harissa on the toast and sit the egg halves on top. Season the eggs with flaked sea salt and a pinch of black pepper and serve immediately.

As a dip for smashed potatoes

You can dial down the fiery nature of the harissa by mixing it with mayo and this makes a great dip. I made these incredibly moreish potatoes for my friend Jemma when she came to stay and let's just say she was lucky to find any left by the time she arrived.

Serves 4 (or just me)
as a side dish or snack

—

500g new potatoes, scrubbed
2½ tbsp olive oil
1 tsp ground cumin
3 tbsp mayonnaise
1 tbsp Green Harissa (see recipe, pages 138–9)
flaked sea salt and freshly ground black pepper

Preheat the oven to 250°C/480°F/Gas mark 9.

Put the potatoes into a medium saucepan. Cover with cold water, add a pinch of flaked sea salt and bring to the boil over a high heat. Turn the heat down to medium, cover and simmer for 15 minutes until tender, then drain.

Drizzle a baking tray with ½ tablespoon of the olive oil and spread the cooked potatoes out evenly. Using a potato masher or the bottom of a jug, gently crush each potato until it is about half its original thickness, drizzle with the remaining 2 tablespoons of olive oil and sprinkle with the cumin, a pinch of flaked sea salt and a grind of black pepper. Bake on the top shelf of the oven for 20 minutes until golden brown. The bases should be crispy, and the middles should be soft and fluffy.

Put the mayonnaise into a small bowl, add the harissa and stir well to combine. Place on a serving platter with the cooked potatoes.

Roasted butternut squash

recipe overleaf

Roasted butternut squash

Having a tub of roasted squash in the fridge can lead to a multitude of meals. Use the cubes in a salad, in a Buddha bowl, as part of an antipasti platter or in one of the three following recipes. I've suggested butternut squash as it is by far the most widely available squash, as well as being reliable in its texture and sweetness. Other varieties of squash and pumpkin can, of course, be cooked in the same way, as can sweet potato. Seasoning the squash well with salt and pepper and adding the pul biber balances out its natural sweetness and is essential, in my opinion.

Makes approx. 900g

—

2 medium butternut squash,
   peeled and cut into 2cm dice
   (approx. 1kg prepared weight)
1 level tsp pul biber (mild Turkish
   chilli flakes)
olive oil
flaked sea salt and freshly ground
   black pepper

Preheat the oven to 200°C/400°F/Gas mark 6.

Put the butternut squash cubes into a large bowl.
Add the pul biber, 2 tablespoons of olive oil, a level
teaspoon of flaked sea salt and a generous pinch of
black pepper and mix well with your hands, making
sure the squash is evenly coated. Tip into a large
roasting tray and roast for 35 minutes in the hot oven,
tossing halfway through.

To store
Once roasted this will keep well in a sealable container
in the fridge for 3 days. Bring to room temperature if
eating it cold.

As a pasta sauce with ricotta

An extremely quick and simple sauce that you can make while your pasta cooks. It's brilliantly creamy (a whole tub of ricotta will do that) and the creaminess, along with the sweetness of the roasted squash, is balanced by the peppery rocket and the heat of the chilli flakes. I love the garlic and the basil coming through in the sauce, and the few extra basil leaves served on top will release their pungent fragrance as the hot pasta warms them up. A midweek feast for all the senses. You can also serve the roasted squash sauce as a dip for a crudité platter, baked toasts, crisps or toasted pitta.

Serves 4, very generously
—

500g fusilli
400g Roasted Butternut Squash (see recipe, pages 148–9)
1 x 250g tub ricotta
1 garlic clove, peeled and grated or finely chopped
1 bunch of basil leaves (approx. 25g), picked
20g rocket
flaked sea salt and freshly ground black pepper
extra-virgin olive oil, to serve
Parmesan cheese, to serve
pinch of pul biber (mild Turkish chilli flakes), to serve

Cook the pasta according to packet instructions then drain, reserving the cooking water.

While the pasta is cooking, make the sauce. Put the roasted butternut squash into a food processor along with the ricotta, garlic and most of the basil. Blitz until the sauce is totally smooth, adding a splash of water to loosen if needed. Season to taste with flaked sea salt and black pepper and tip the sauce into a large saucepan. Place over a medium-low heat to warm through.

When the pasta is cooked and drained, tip into the sauce, adding 100ml of the reserved pasta water little by little until the pasta is well coated in sauce.

Toss the pasta and the sauce together, divide between 4 plates and top each one with a handful of rocket, the reserved basil leaves, a drizzle of olive oil, a grating of Parmesan and a pinch of pul biber.

Spiced squash and coconut soup

This easy soup only takes a little longer to whip up than heating up a carton of shop-bought stuff. If you want to make the same soup but are starting with uncooked squash, follow the same instructions but after adding the squash, throw in a cupful of vegetable stock and simmer for 15 minutes to soften the veg before continuing.

Serves 2, generously

—

1 tbsp pumpkin seeds
1 tbsp olive oil
1 medium onion, peeled and
    roughly chopped
1 garlic clove, peeled and
    finely chopped
1 tsp ground cumin
½ tsp turmeric
300g Roasted Butternut Squash
    (see recipe, pages 148–9)
1 x 400g tin coconut milk
¼ red chilli, finely sliced, to serve
1 sprig of coriander, leaves picked,
    to serve

Toast the pumpkin seeds in a dry pan over a medium heat for 1–2 minutes until starting to burst, shaking the pan often.

Heat the olive oil in a saucepan over a medium heat. Add the onion and cook for 5 minutes until softened, stirring occasionally. Add the garlic and cook for a further 30 seconds. Add the cumin and turmeric, stir and cook for another minute before adding the cooked butternut squash and stirring it all together for another minute. Turn the heat down to low, add the coconut milk (reserving a little to garnish) and cook for 1 minute before blitzing with a hand-held blender until totally smooth.

To serve, drizzle the reserved coconut milk over the surface of the soup and sprinkle with the pumpkin seeds, chilli slices and the coriander.

Bruschetta with feta and pumpkin seeds

Leftover roast veggies on toast with the addition of a little cheese and some seeds is a really basic but brilliant way to make a quick snack or light lunch. Use up herbs, utilise your spice stores, play around. This is a lovely combo when you've got cooked squash to use, but would work equally well with all sorts of other cooked veg such as aubergine, peppers — even peas.

Serves 2, as a snack

—

4 x 1cm-thick slices of ciabatta
    or sourdough
olive oil
1 tsp pumpkin seeds
400g Roasted Butternut Squash
    (see recipe, pages 148–9)
1 heaped tsp finely chopped
    flat-leaf parsley
20g feta cheese
pinch of smoked paprika
a squeeze of lemon juice or a splash
    of sherry vinegar (optional)

Preheat the oven to 180°C/350°F/Gas mark 4.

Lay the bread on a baking tray, drizzle both sides with 1 teaspoon of olive oil and bake in the oven for 5–10 minutes until golden brown and toasted.

Meanwhile, toast the pumpkin seeds in a dry pan over a medium heat for 1–2 minutes until starting to burst, shaking the pan often.

Put the Roasted butternut squash into a small bowl, add the parsley and use a fork to crush into a rough paste.

Remove the toasts from the oven, divide the crushed squash between them and crumble over the feta. Top with the pumpkin seeds and a sprinkling of smoked paprika and add a little squeeze of lemon or a splash of vinegar if you like. Serve immediately.

Roasted spiced plums

recipe overleaf

Roasted spiced plums

The ease:result ratio of this recipe is well out of whack. You simply sling the plums in the oven, having spent all of 1 minute halving them and sprinkling them with a few things. Half an hour later, the most glorious treats appear that you can use in all sorts of ways. I have a big jar of the cinnamon sugar made up and ready to go, and I've got my PB for putting it together down to sub-30 seconds. Make loads, it goes fast.

—

salted butter, for greasing
6 ripe plums, halved and stoned
1 heaped tbsp cinnamon sugar
    (see recipe, page 107)
¼ tsp ground mixed spice
6 star anise

Preheat the oven to 200°C/400°F/Gas mark 6.

Grease a 16 x 24cm ovenproof baking dish with the butter. Place the plums cut-side up in the baking dish. Sprinkle with 1 heaped tablespoon of cinnamon sugar (if you don't have this made up, use 1 tablespoon of sugar to 1 teaspoon of ground cinnamon), the mixed spice and the star anise.

Roast for 30 minutes on the middle shelf of the oven, then remove and leave to cool for 5 minutes. Remove the star anise. You will find there is a lovely plummy syrup in the base of the dish which you can spoon over the plums when serving.

To store
The cooked plums will keep in a sealable container in the fridge for a couple of days.

In a cookie dough crumble

As the name suggests, the topping of this easy crumble is half oat crumble, half cookie dough mix. Need I say more?

Serves 2

—

1 batch of Roasted Spiced Plums
   (see recipe, pages 156–7)
30g soft brown sugar
25g salted butter, chilled and cubed
15g plain flour
15g rolled porridge oats
1 pinch of flaked sea salt

Preheat the oven to 200°C/400°F/Gas mark 6.

Split the plums and their syrup between 2 ramekins or small baking dishes and set aside.

Combine the sugar, butter and flour in a bowl and rub together with your fingertips until breadcrumb-like in texture. Add the oats and flaked sea salt and mix well. Top the plums with the crumble mixture, sit on a baking tray and place in the centre of the oven for 20 minutes. Leave for 5 minutes before serving. Beware, the centres will be extremely hot.

With Greek-style yoghurt and toasted pistachios

Serves 4

—

3 tbsp unsalted pistachios, shelled
8 heaped tbsp Greek-style yoghurt
1 batch of Roasted Spiced Plums
    (see recipe, pages 156–7)

Soft, sweet, spiced, roasted plums, resting on a dollop of creamy yoghurt and sprinkled with nuts. Breakfast, snack, pudding – I could happily eat this simple but delicious combo at any time of day.

Toast the pistachios in a dry frying pan over a medium heat until starting to brown. This should only take a minute or so. Tip them onto a chopping board, leave to cool then roughly chop.

Divide the yoghurt between 4 bowls. Top with the roasted plums (along with their syrupy roasting juices) and finish with a sprinkling of chopped pistachios.

Spiced plum and soured cream upside-down cake

Image p. 247

I love an upside-down cake. The excitement when you take a very plain-looking cake out of the oven, flip it over and peel off the paper to reveal the pattern created by the fruit never gets old.

I'd been wanting to find a way to use a jar of interesting-looking spice mix in my cupboard for ages. A Hogweed spice blend I bought at Abergavenny Food Festival is stunning and went brilliantly with the roasted plums but is not easy to find. Grab some if you can, but all sorts of other things would work well here. I've suggested ginger or cinnamon, but a mixture of the two or even some cardamom would be great too. You can of course use other fruits in this recipe.

cont.

Serves 8–10

—

85g salted butter, softened,
    plus extra for greasing
150g caster sugar
2 free-range eggs, beaten
140g plain flour, sifted
½ lemon, zested
100g soured cream
1 pinch of flaked sea salt
½ tsp baking powder
1 tsp ground spice such as ginger,
    cinnamon or Hogweed spice blend
    (or a mixture)
1 batch of Roasted Spiced Plums
    (see recipe, pages 156–7)
2 tbsp unsalted pistachios,
    shelled (optional)
crème fraîche, softly whipped
    cream or ice cream, to serve

Preheat the oven to 180°C/350°F/Gas mark 4. Grease a 20cm round loose-bottomed cake tin with butter and line with greaseproof paper.

Cream the butter and sugar together until light and fluffy. Add half the beaten egg and a spoonful of the flour. Beat well until fully combined, then add the remaining egg along with another spoonful of the flour. Add the lemon zest and soured cream and mix well. Mix the salt, baking powder and spices with the remaining flour, then add a spoonful at a time to the creamed butter and sugar mixture, using a rubber spatula to carefully cut through and fold into the mixture, being careful not to overmix.

Sit the plums cut-side down in the base of the lined tin and spoon the batter carefully over the top. Smooth the surface evenly and bake in the centre of the oven for 35–40 minutes, or until a knife inserted into the centre comes out clean. Cool for 15 minutes before inverting. Peel off the greaseproof paper, sprinkle the pistachios over the surface and serve with cream, crème fraîche or ice cream.

This cake keeps well for a couple of days, as it's very moist and dense. Keep it wrapped in its paper and inside an airtight container.

Menus

Try individual dishes or the whole menu, it's up to you

This final chapter contains eight separate full menus, all designed to help you put on a proper spread.

From two people to loads – our modern lives demand more ways of feeding guests than the 'dinner parties' of old. I like to find a happy balance between things that can be prepared in advance and a bit of simple, last-minute stuff. I want things that aren't going to stress me out. I want to use produce that is easy to get hold of and maybe a few bits that might be new discoveries for my guests. I want to wow them with the food but also with the fact I'm not having a breakdown trying to get it all on the table. There's plenty of drink suggestions too (some boozy, some not).

Try individual dishes or make the whole menu, it's up to you. Now, who are you going to invite?

Baby shower brunch for a crowd with breast-feeding mums who could eat a horse

Bagels, smoked salmon and caper cream cheese

A big pile of bagels. If you're lucky enough to live near a bakery making fresh bagels, that's your best option. Remember that fresh bagels freeze really well, so if you find yourself on Brick Lane, in London, for example, buy a load, slice them open and put them in a sealable freezer bag. Chuck them in the freezer and you'll find they defrost within a couple of hours at room temperature. If I've got good, proper bagels, I'd never, ever toast them. If I've got supermarket bagels, I'd never, ever serve them untoasted. But that's just me. Do whatever you like.

Serves 10
—

2 lemons
250–500g smoked salmon (depending on how generous you're feeling)
10 bagels
flaked sea salt and freshly ground black pepper

For the caper cream cheese
1 x 280g tub cream cheese
1 x 200g tub cottage cheese
8 tbsp baby capers, drained
4 tbsp finely chopped dill
4 tbsp very finely diced red onion

For the caper cream cheese, blend the cream cheese and cottage cheese together in a food processor. Stir through the other ingredients. Season to taste with flaked sea salt and black pepper and chill for at least an hour before serving.

Cut the lemons into wedges and serve with the salmon (allow 25–50g of salmon per person) but don't squeeze over the lemon juice before serving – it'll discolour the salmon and make it tough. Put a pepper mill nearby too.

Slice open the bagels and pile on a big platter, then decide whether you want to pre-fill them so your guests can just grab one with one hand (best if you're doing a standing-up party) or serve the salmon and caper cream cheese separately and let people fill their own.

Pea frittata bites

Every baby I've ever met loves peas, pesto and pasta and there are often leftovers in the fridge. This is a good way of using everything up, and putting pasta in a frittata is actually an authentic thing. Honestly. The size and shape of these mini frittatas make them perfect for little hands, but they are also really delicious for adults. If you want to make a big baked frittata and cut it up, line a cake tin with buttered greaseproof paper and follow the same directions, cooking until the centre is set.

Makes 12

—

2 tsp unsalted butter, plus extra for greasing
6 free-range eggs
150g frozen peas, defrosted
100g cooked penne (or any cooked pasta), cut into 1cm rings
3 tbsp pesto (see recipe, page 52 or use shop-bought)
50g Cheddar cheese, grated

Preheat the oven to 180°C/350°F/Gas mark 4 and grease a 12-hole cake or muffin tin with butter.

Crack the eggs into a large bowl, mix all the remaining ingredients into the eggs until fully combined, then distribute evenly between the 12 holes.

Bake in the centre of the hot oven for 15 minutes then remove and leave to cool for 5 minutes before removing from the tin and serving hot, warm or at room temperature.

Grapefruit soda (with gin if you like)

I created this recipe when I had a bald, zested grapefruit left over from making the shortbread on page 174. Chop it all up roughly and turn it into homemade Ting! It's fab too with rum or gin if you want to make it boozy.

Serves 10
—

2 regular or pink grapefruits, approx. 500g (you can use the grapefruit that has already been zested and used for the shortbread recipe on page 174)
100g white caster sugar
plenty of ice
a few sprigs of mint
soda or sparkling water

You can use any citrus here; it's a great way to use up zested or halved fruit sitting in the fridge. Make the total up to 500g with lemons/limes/satsumas, etc.

Wash the grapefruits and hack them up, flesh, zest and all. Put the grapefruit in a small saucepan with the sugar and 150ml of water. Place over a medium heat until the sugar dissolves. Bring to a boil, then turn the heat down to medium-low and simmer for 5 minutes, stirring occasionally and mashing the grapefruit with the back of a spoon. Remove from the heat, use a potato masher to crush it all together and leave to cool. Strain the mixture through a sieve into a bowl, using a spoon to squeeze out as much syrup as possible.

To serve, fill a jug with ice, add a few sprigs of mint, pour over the grapefruit syrup, and dilute it to taste (I suggest a ratio of 1:4), by topping it up with soda or sparkling water. Stir well to mix.

Rose and honey still lemonade

This uses honey rather than sugar, which goes beautifully with the rose flavour. A really pretty, delicate drink.

Serves 8
—

160g runny honey
6 heaped tbsp dried rose petals
120ml freshly squeezed lemon juice (or more to taste)
plenty of ice

Pour 1.5 litres of water into a large saucepan, add the honey and bring to the boil over a medium heat. Add the rose petals, breaking them up as you go, then remove from the heat. Cover, leave to cool at room temperature, then put in the fridge and leave to chill for 2 hours. Strain through a fine sieve into a jug. Stir in half the lemon juice and taste. Add more lemon juice to your liking and serve in glasses over plenty of ice.

Earl Grey, almond and grapefruit shortbread

Makes approx. 25

—

2 tsp loose-leaf Earl Grey tea
50g caster sugar
1 grapefruit, zested, plus 2 tsp juice
   (use the rest of the juice in the
   Grapefruit soda recipe, page 172)
100g ground almonds
100g polenta
70g salted butter, cut into
   1cm cubes

These little biscuits are incredibly moreish and keep well so you can make them a couple of days in advance. They are also gluten-free and contain just 2g of sugar per biscuit.

Tip the tea, sugar and grapefruit zest into a food processor and whizz for a couple of seconds. Add the ground almonds and polenta and whizz again. Then add the butter and whizz until the mixture has the consistency of wet sand. Pour in the grapefruit juice, blitz for a couple of seconds, then tip into a large bowl.

Lay an A4 piece of cling film out on a work surface. Use your hands to scoop up approximately half the mixture and squeeze it into a sausage shape. Lay the sausage on the longest edge of the cling film nearest to you. Roll up into a tight sausage-shaped log about 3–4cm in diameter and twist both ends of the cling film to compress the mixture. Repeat with the other half of the mixture and put both dough 'sausages' into the fridge to chill for 1 hour.

Preheat the oven to 150°C/300°F/Gas mark 2. Line a baking tray with greaseproof paper, unwrap the 'sausages' of dough and very carefully slice into 1cm-thick discs. The mixture will be delicate and crumbly and you may need to reshape the biscuits as you go. Lay the slices out on the prepared tray, leaving a space of about 2.5cm between them as the biscuits will spread a little during baking.

Bake for 15 minutes in the centre of the hot oven until the shortbreads are 'blonde' with a hint of tan. Remove from the oven and leave to cool on the baking tray for 5 minutes. Using a palette knife, carefully move them to a wire rack to cool completely. As with all biscuits, these will firm up once cooled. They keep well in a sealable container for a few days.

Berries and yoghurt with date syrup and pumpkin seeds

A big bowl of fruit is a really lovely addition to any brunch menu. Allow a small handful of berries per person – a mixture of blueberries, raspberries and strawberries is my personal favourite. Serve alongside a big bowlful of Greek-style yoghurt. I like to swirl date or maple syrup through the yoghurt and sprinkle with toasted pumpkin seeds.

Blueberry and mint fizz

This blueberry syrup makes a great topping for ice cream, as well as being the base of this sparkling concoction. This is a delicious alcohol-free drink, perfect for expectant mums. You can make it in advance and it will keep in a jar in the fridge for weeks. Maybe make extra, fill some little bottles and give to guests to take home.

Serves 6

—

plenty of ice
1 litre sparkling water
1 small bunch of mint (approx. 20g), leaves picked

For the blueberry syrup
150g blueberries
200g caster sugar

To make the syrup, simply put the blueberries and sugar into a medium saucepan with 250ml of water. Bring to the boil over a high heat, then reduce the heat to medium-low and simmer for 15 minutes. Strain through a fine sieve and keep the syrup in a sealed jar in the fridge (you'll have enough for approximately 20 servings).

Fill a jug a third-full with ice. Pour in the fizzy water, then drizzle in 6 tablespoons of the blueberry syrup and use a long spoon to stir and combine everything. Gently scrunch the mint leaves to bruise them and release their flavour and add to the jug. Make sure the blueberry syrup is fully dissolved before serving.

Lunch for six when sandwiches just won't do

Crudité platter

a mixture of raw, crunchy veg (see right)
a bowl of nice olives, to serve
breadsticks or crackers, to serve

My favourite combo of crudités:

+ celery, cut into batons

+ radishes, large ones halved, small ones left whole

+ cucumber, cut into batons, seedy core removed

+ cherry tomatoes, large ones halved, small ones left whole

+ endive/chicory, leaves separated and left whole

+ carrots, peeled and cut into batons

+ broccoli or cauliflower, cut into florets, stalks peeled and cut into discs

+ sugar snap peas, left whole

+ red, yellow or orange pepper, deseeded and cut into batons

Cottage cheese with za'atar

150g Greek-style yoghurt
200g cottage cheese
1 tsp za'atar (see recipe, page 94)
flaked sea salt and freshly ground black pepper

Combine the yoghurt and cottage cheese and season to taste with flaked sea salt and black pepper. Transfer to a small serving bowl and sprinkle the za'atar across the surface.

Plum drinking vinegar

The word 'shrub' comes from the Arabic word *sharab*, meaning 'to drink'. Think of them as grown-up cordials or squash – made with vinegar, sugar and fruit. You mix them with water (still or sparkling) for a refreshing drink, balanced between sharp and sweet.

Makes approx. 750ml

—

500g plums, halved and stoned
500g caster sugar
5cm piece of root ginger (unpeeled), sliced 2mm thick
1 tsp pink peppercorns
200ml apple cider vinegar (look for one that has 'with the mother' on the label)

I first tried drinking vinegars, AKA shrubs, at a restaurant called Bellita in Bristol, where Kate Hawkings makes her own out of all sorts of seasonal fruit. I felt absolutely awful one day but was determined not to miss an event happening at Bellita that I knew lots of my mates would be going to. I had the worst stomach ache and definitely did not feel like drinking. Kate made me a shrub and I instantly felt better. This could well have been an utter fluke but it made me sit up and notice these new-to-me drinks.

This recipe uses apple cider vinegar, which is widely heralded as a miracle ingredient. It's apparently good for so many things – there's hundreds of books called things like *Apple Cider Vinegar, The Miracle Cure!* and *101 Ways With Apple Cider Vinegar.* I have not read these books so cannot comment but I have read a brilliant book called *Ducksoup Cookbook: The Wisdom of Simple Cooking,* which is where I learnt more about these drinking vinegars and how to make my own. This plum version is my fave combo yet.

Put the plums, sugar, 300ml of water and the ginger into a large saucepan over a high heat. Bring to the boil, then turn the heat down to low and simmer for 45 minutes. Add the pink peppercorns and simmer for a further 15 minutes. Remove from the heat, cover and leave to one side to cool for 8 hours or overnight.

Add the vinegar, then cover and leave to one side in a cool, dry place for 24 hours. Strain slowly through a fine mesh or very fine sieve into a jug and store in the fridge in a sealed bottle. Serve diluted 1:4 with fizzy water, over ice.

Beetroot pickled eggs

You can make pickled eggs from scratch or you can cheat and do it like this. We use pickled beetroot at my café and get through loads of it, so there's always plenty of beetrooty brine that would otherwise get wasted. We boiled some eggs one day and put them in the finished jars and a day later — ta-da! Pink eggs. I once made hundreds of these for a wedding buffet and I'm still not sick of them. Use good-quality eggs with really golden yolks to get the best contrast with the pink.

1 very large jar of pickled beetroots
(sliced, whole or baby — any type)
as many hard-boiled free-range
chicken or quail eggs as will fit in
your jar, peeled

Once you've finished eating all the beetroot from the jar, keep the pink pickling liquid and add the boiled eggs to it, ensuring all the eggs are covered. Leave for 1–4 days before eating.

After 1 day, the eggs will have a distinct pink outer ring — longer and the entire white will go pink. Either way is fine, it's just a matter of which look you want to go for.

Beetroot tzatziki

½ tsp cumin seeds
1 raw beetroot, peeled and grated
150g Greek-style yoghurt
½–1 garlic clove, peeled
and crushed
1 heaped tsp finely chopped dill
1 tsp extra-virgin olive oil, plus a little
extra to finish
sea salt and freshly ground
black pepper

Toast the cumin seeds in a dry pan over a medium heat for 1 minute until they release an amazing smell, shaking the pan often. Remove from the heat and combine with all the other ingredients in a bowl; stir well. Season to taste with salt and pepper and finish with a slick of your best olive oil.

Warm pitta, yoghurt and chickpea salad

3 large pitta breads
olive oil
1 x 400g tin chickpeas
1 tsp ground cumin
200g Greek-style yoghurt
1½ tbsp tahini
½ lemon, juiced
1 garlic clove, peeled and crushed
    or finely grated
flaked sea salt and freshly ground
    black pepper

To garnish
2 tbsp pine nuts
25g feta cheese
1 small bunch of mint (approx. 20g),
    leaves picked
3 radishes, very finely sliced
1 big pinch of smoked paprika
1 big pinch of sumac
argan oil or extra-virgin olive oil
1 small handful of Middle Eastern
    pickled turnips or beetroot, cut
    into bite-size pieces
smoked sea salt (optional)

Preheat the oven to 180°C/350°F/Gas mark 4.

Put the pitta bread on a baking tray, drizzle both sides with olive oil and bake in the oven for 10 minutes.

Tip the chickpeas and their liquid (reserving 3 tablespoons of the liquid), into a saucepan and place over a medium heat to warm through. Add the cumin and 2 teaspoons of olive oil, stir well and reduce the heat to low while you make the rest of the salad.

Put the yoghurt into a large bowl, add the tahini, lemon juice, garlic and the reserved 3 tablespoons of liquid from the chickpeas and whisk well.

Pour 2cm water into a medium-sized saucepan and bring to a simmer over a medium-low heat. Sit the bowl of yoghurt mixture over the pan to gently heat. Whisk regularly so the mixture is warmed through and the flavours are blended together; this will take about 5 minutes.

Cut the pitta breads into 2–3cm squares and separate the two layers. Keep a handful of the pitta squares to one side for garnishing and spread the remaining bread out on a platter or put into a serving bowl. Drizzle a couple of ladles of the warm chickpea cooking broth over the bread until they are just soaked.

Strain the chickpeas and pour them over the soaked bread. Using a large spoon, spoon the warmed yoghurt mixture over the chickpeas and gently fold the layers together.

Heat 1 teaspoon of olive oil in a frying pan over a medium heat and fry the pine nuts until golden brown, shaking the pan often. Keep an eye on them, as they will burn easily.

Scoop the pine nuts out of the frying pan and put to one side, then add the reserved bread to the frying pan and toast until golden and extra crispy.

cont.

Spoon the pine nuts over the surface of the
chickpeas and yoghurt, crumble over the feta,
scatter the mint on top, add the radish slices,
the crispy bread, smoked paprika and sumac,
and drizzle the whole lot with some argan oil
or extra-virgin olive oil. Scatter over the pickled
turnips or beetroot, then season with the smoked
salt (if using) or flaked sea salt and a pinch of
black pepper.

Kuku sabzi

Kuku sabzi is a Persian-style herb frittata. It's densely green, punctuated with little pops of sharp barberries and lovely toasted walnuts.

30g walnuts, roughly chopped
6 free-range eggs, beaten
70g Greek-style yoghurt
½ tsp turmeric
2 heaped tsp flaked sea salt
1 small bunch of flat-leaf parsley
   (approx. 20g), leaves picked and
   roughly chopped
1 small bunch of coriander
   (approx. 20g), leaves picked and
   roughly chopped
1 bunch of dill (approx. 20g), leaves
   picked and roughly chopped
1 bunch of chives (approx. 20g),
   finely chopped
20g dried barberries (available
   from Middle Eastern grocers,
   or you can substitute 20g finely
   chopped dried cranberries plus
   a grating of lemon zest)
2 spring onions, finely sliced
30g rocket, roughly chopped
freshly ground black pepper

Preheat the oven to 180°C/350°F/Gas mark 4.

Toast the walnuts in a dry pan over a medium heat for 1–2 minutes, until golden, shaking the pan often.

Line a 20cm loose-bottomed cake tin with greaseproof paper. The easiest way to do this is to tear off a square of paper a little bigger than you need and screw it into a tight ball. You will find that when you open the paper and put it in the tin, it will stay put without popping out.

Put the beaten eggs and yoghurt into a large bowl. Add the turmeric, salt and a good pinch of black pepper and whisk well. Add all the other ingredients and stir well. Pour into the lined cake tin and immediately stick it in the hot oven to bake for 30 minutes.

Remove from the oven and leave to cool slightly before slicing and serving. The kuku sabzi is best eaten at room temperature and will keep for up to 3 days in the fridge.

Tips for leftover herbs and leaves

There's an amazing pesto in *Fast Days & Feast Days* which uses up basil and rocket and uses walnuts too. Remember, leftover greens of any kind can be slung into a frittata.

Roasted broccoli and chilli

Just like cauliflower, broccoli benefits massively from roasting. This is a great side dish that goes with all sorts of things. Try serving it with noodles or rice and an egg, throw it into a salad or mix it into pasta or a frittata.

2 heads of broccoli
1½ tbsp olive oil
½ red chilli, finely sliced
flaked sea salt and freshly
    ground black pepper

Preheat the oven to 200°C/400°F/Gas mark 6.

Cut the broccoli into florets, peel the stalk and cut into ½cm discs. Tip all the broccoli into a large bowl, add the olive oil, season generously with flaked sea salt and freshly ground black pepper and toss everything together so that the broccoli is well coated.

Tip on to a baking tray in a single layer (you may need to use 2 trays) and roast in the oven for approximately 20 minutes until the edges of the broccoli florets begin to char. Tip into a serving bowl and serve scattered with the finely sliced red chilli.

Dinner for four when you want to show off a bit but not stress

Seared scallops with cauliflower purée, capers and pine nuts

The purée can be made in advance and the scallops take only a few minutes to cook – perfect dinner party fodder. Once the purée is ready it all comes together really quickly. It's essential that you warm plates for this dish before you start doing anything else. You can do this in a low oven or put them in a sink full of very hot water then dry them.

For the cauliflower purée
60g salted butter
240g cauliflower, roughly chopped
1 tsp medium curry powder
120ml whole milk
flaked sea salt and freshly ground
    black pepper

For the scallops
12 scallops, roe left on or
    off, your preference
olive oil
1 knob of salted butter
4 tsp pine nuts
4 tsp baby capers, drained

To make the purée, melt the butter in a saucepan over a medium heat. Add the cauliflower and cook for 6–8 minutes until the cauliflower starts to brown, stirring occasionally. Stir in the curry powder then add the milk. Bring to a simmer then turn the heat down to low, cover and simmer for 8 minutes. Remove from the heat and set aside, still covered, for 1 minute.

Tip the contents of the pan into a food processor and blitz until completely smooth. You can do this stage up to 3 days in advance then keep the purée covered in the fridge until needed.

Return the purée to a small pan over a low heat to gently reheat, stirring occasionally. Season to taste with flaked sea salt and black pepper and keep warm while you cook the scallops.

Lay the scallops out on a plate, trim off any tough sinewy bits, then pat dry with kitchen paper. Sprinkle both sides with flaked sea salt and black pepper. Heat your largest frying pan over a high heat and when hot, add the oil, then the butter.

cont.

Place the first scallop at the top of your pan (at 12 o'clock) and hold it down for a couple of seconds to encourage as much surface area to brown as possible. Do not shake the pan or move them once they are in; you want them to form a golden crust. Work your way around the pan clockwise until all the scallops are in. When you get back to the first one (at 12 o'clock), lift it gently and check that it has a nice golden crust. Gently flip it over and work your way round clockwise until they are all turned over. They only need 1–2 minutes cooking in total (30 seconds to 1 minute on each side).

Lay your warm plates out and divide the spiced cauliflower purée between them. When the scallops are cooked, sit them on top of the purée then immediately add the pine nuts and the capers to the frying pan; use a spatula to scrape up all the brown butter and warm everything through for a few seconds. The capers will start to puff up and the pine nuts will very quickly turn golden.

Carefully spoon this mixture over the scallops and serve immediately.

Smoked haddock tart

This tart was the result of a *Supermarket-Sweep*-style dash around Stockbridge Farmers' Market in Edinburgh. A seasonal haul that immediately suggested a tart. Scottish produce is so brilliant and that market has a particularly good fish stall. You don't need to muck around when you've got such great food to play with. You can use either a fluted 10 x 32cm rectangular tart tin or a fluted 20cm round tart tin for this.

For the pastry
225g plain flour, plus extra
    for dusting
100g salted butter, chilled, cubed,
    plus extra for greasing
2 separate free-range egg yolks,
    each beaten

For the filling
200g crème fraîche
2 free-range eggs
2 spring onions, very finely sliced
2 tsp wholegrain mustard
40g watercress, roughly chopped
250g smoked haddock, skin removed
    and flesh roughly chopped
flaked sea salt and freshly ground
    black pepper

buttered new potatoes, to serve
    (optional)

Sift the flour into a large bowl. Add a pinch of flaked sea salt and the butter and rub with your fingertips until the mixture resembles fine breadcrumbs. Put one of the beaten egg yolks in a small bowl, add 2 tablespoons of cold water and mix well. Add 2 tablespoons of the mixture to the flour and mix with the blade of a knife to form a firm dough, adding more of the mixture to bring the dough together if needed.

Bring together with your hands to form a ball. Knead briefly on a clean flour-dusted work surface, then wrap in cling film and chill in the fridge for 30 minutes. Remove the pastry from the fridge and leave at room temperature for 5 minutes. Grease your tart tin.

Dust a clean work surface with flour and roll the pastry out into a rectangle or circle, depending on the shape of your tin, about 1–2mm thick and larger than your tin.

Lay the pastry into the greased tin and press into the fluted edges. Make sure the pastry is pushed right in and is of even thickness all the way round. Trim off any excess by rolling your rolling pin across the top of the tin and use the excess pastry to plug any tears or gaps (don't worry, this often happens). Use a fork to prick a few holes in the base of the pastry, then chill in the fridge for 30 minutes. This is an essential stage to stop your pastry shrinking, so do not rush it.

cont.

Preheat the oven to 180°C/350°F/Gas mark 4. Scrunch up some greaseproof paper, open up, smooth out and put into the chilled pastry case, then fill with baking beans or raw rice and bake for 15 minutes. Remove from the oven, take out the paper and beans or rice, then brush the pastry with the remaining beaten egg yolk. Return to the oven for 5 minutes.

To make the filling, in a large jug, whisk together the crème fraîche, the 2 eggs, spring onions, wholegrain mustard, a pinch of black pepper and the watercress.

Spread the haddock over the pastry base and pour over the mixture. Bake for 20–25 minutes until the filling is set and the top is starting to brown. Serve hot or cold, but it is best eaten with buttered new potatoes and Stephen Fry cabbage.

Stephen Fry cabbage

Cooking greens this way (steaming and frying) means you'll end up with greens, not greys, and they'll have good bite to them. 'Steam and fry' became 'Stephen Fry' at my café as a joke after a misheard instruction and it's stuck. All greens are better when you've Stephen Fry'd them.

1 Savoy cabbage
50g salted butter
flaked sea salt and freshly
   ground black pepper

Remove any grotty outer leaves from the cabbage. Halve from root to tip and cut out the core. Shred each half so you have a big pile of cabbage ribbons approximately ½cm wide. Wash and shake dry. Do not spin dry – you want the cabbage to be a little wet.

Heat a large wok or your largest frying pan over a high heat. Add the butter and, when it's melted, throw in the cabbage. Stir-fry for a couple of minutes until completely hot, then remove from the heat, cover with foil and leave to steam until ready to serve. It'll stay hot for quite a long time. Season well with flaked sea salt and black pepper before serving.

Pre-dinner cocktails

GE&T

50ml gin
50ml elderflower cordial
200ml tonic water
1 lemon wedge

Pour the gin, cordial and tonic into an ice-filled glass and stir. Squeeze in the lemon juice and serve.

Rose vermouth and tonic

75ml rose vermouth
100ml tonic water
1 slice of orange
    or grapefruit

Combine all the ingredients in a glass over ice.

This makes a delicious lower alcohol option if you change the ratio of vermouth to tonic. Try 50ml:200ml (that's approximately half as much alcohol as a 50ml:200ml G&T)

Spiced plums with Greek-style yoghurt and toasted pistachios

See recipe, page 160.

Kitchen table dinner for four, thinking of Jerez

Marcona almonds and fat green olives

Marcona almonds are imported from Spain and are always my top choice for eating with a glass of Fino. They are rounder and fatter than regular (often Californian) almonds and the texture is closer to a macadamia. The skins are blanched off then the almonds are roasted in olive oil and sprinkled with flaked sea salt. They are more expensive than normal almonds but, in my opinion, worth every penny.

I prefer big fat green olives to any other and the ones I get really excited about are the Spanish 'Gordal' olives. You can buy them (and the Marconas) from Spanish delis and online from brindisa.com.

Padrón peppers

This is one of the simplest tapas dishes you can make. Really quick and always popular. The saying goes that you'll get a really hot one in every 10 (or 15 according to some people), but I've eaten hundreds and have only ever had one scorcher.

120g Padrón peppers
1 tsp olive oil
flaked sea salt

Simply wash and dry the peppers and leave them whole. Heat the olive oil in a large frying pan and fry the peppers until blistered all over. This will only take 5–10 minutes. Tip them into a serving bowl and sprinkle with plenty of flaked sea salt.

Hake traybake

This is a brill, easy, one-pan hake dish that includes elements of both romesco sauce and panzanella salad. Confession time: I thought I'd create a delicious nutty crumb mixture to make a crust on the fish. I did, it was delicious, and then I discovered I'd basically made picada, a classic Catalan sauce. Oh well. It's delicious.

1 ramiro pepper (long pointed red pepper)
1 red onion, peeled and cut into wedges
1 tbsp olive oil
400g ripe tomatoes (a mixture of colours and sizes is great but use whatever you can find)
50g black olives, stone in
60g stale bread (ciabatta is perfect), torn into bite-size pieces
200g passata
a few sprigs of thyme, leaves picked
1 small handful of basil leaves, torn (plus a few small leaves to garnish)
1 tbsp red wine vinegar
4 hake fillets, skin on
pinch of sweet smoked paprika
pinch of pul biber (mild Turkish chilli flakes)
flaked sea salt and freshly ground black pepper

For the crumb
40g fresh breadcrumbs
40g blanched almonds
40g whole hazelnuts
½ a small bunch of flat-leaf parsley (approx. 10g), leaves picked
2 tbsp olive oil
2 garlic cloves, peeled and roughly chopped

Preheat the oven to 180°C/350°F/Gas mark 4.

Slice the pepper into 1cm-wide rings. Place in a deep 20 x 30cm ovenproof dish with the onion wedges, drizzle over the olive oil and season well with flaked sea salt and black pepper. Roast in the centre of the hot oven for 30 minutes until softened and golden brown.

Once cooked, tip the veg into a large bowl. Halve any cherry tomatoes and quarter any larger tomatoes and add to the roasted veg with the olives, bread, passata, herbs and red wine vinegar. Season and stir it all together to combine. Tip the mixture back into the roasting tin. Lay the hake fillets skin-side down on a plate and sprinkle with the sweet smoked paprika, pul biber and a little flaked sea salt. Lay the fillets skin-side up on top of the tomato mixture and put the whole thing back into the oven for 10 minutes.

Meanwhile, put all the crumb ingredients into a mini food processor and pulse until you have a coarse crumb.

After 10 minutes, remove the fish from the oven, then peel off the skin (it should come off very easily) and discard. Spoon the crumb mixture over the fish fillets and in little piles around them. Place back in the oven to cook for a further 5 minutes. To check the fish is cooked through, use a very sharp knife to cut into the core of the thickest piece; it should be white, opaque and hot. Sprinkle over the remaining basil leaves and serve.

TIP

Passata freezes really well and can be used to make hundreds of different kinds of pasta sauces, soups or pizza toppings.

Freeze your leftover passata

Chicory, orange and almond salad with sherry vinegar, quick pickled onions and parsley

3 heads of chicory
½ red onion, peeled and very
finely sliced
2 tbsp sherry vinegar
1 large orange (regular or
blood orange)
4 tbsp extra-virgin olive oil
½ a small bunch of flat-leaf parsley
(approx. 10g), leaves picked
100g black olives, stoned and
roughly chopped
40g Spanish-style Marcona salted
almonds, roughly chopped
flaked sea salt and freshly ground
black pepper

This salad is one of my favourite combos – it looks massively impressive but is so simple to make. In January and February you'll be able to make this with blood oranges that look extra special but a good big normal orange will more than suffice the rest of the year.

Cut the bases off the chicory heads, separate the leaves, wash and spin dry and put to one side. Put the sliced red onion into a small bowl, add a pinch of flaked sea salt and the sherry vinegar. Mix to combine.

Slice each end off the orange and then with a very sharp knife, working from top to bottom, cut off the peel and the pith following the curve of the fruit. Repeat all the way round the orange. Then hold the naked orange over a serving bowl, and remove the segments by cutting down either side of each membrane, being careful! As you cut the segments out, put them to one side.

When all the segments have been removed, you'll be left with the orange membrane in your hand. Squeeze it hard over the serving bowl to get all the juice; fish out any seeds that have escaped. Now you have the beginning of the dressing in your bowl. Stir in the olive oil, add a pinch of black pepper then, using your fingers, take the sliced red onions out of their vinegary bath, add them to the bowl and whisk everything together. Taste, then add the sherry vinegar from the marinade a little at a time until the dressing has the perfect balance of sour and sweetness. Season with flaked sea salt and black pepper.

Add the orange segments, chicory, parsley and black olives to the bowl. Use your hands to gently toss everything together. Sprinkle some black pepper over the top, scatter with the chopped almonds and serve.

Manchego and membrillo

Manchego is a firm, creamy Spanish cheese, made with sheep's milk. It is nutty and delicious and my favourite match with membrillo, the quince jelly that is so popular in Spain and increasingly easy to get here too. I've made membrillo myself and, although slightly hazardous (the hot bubbling purée is lethal), it's simple – just quince and sugar – and is a great way to preserve fresh quince. Have a go. I recommend the River Cottage 'Quince Cheese' recipe, available on their website. Or buy it. Most large supermarkets stock it now.

Cut the Manchego into 5mm-thick slices – enough for 4 people – and arrange on a plate. Serve with the membrillo and your choice of crackers. I think classic water biscuits work best here.

A glass of PX

A glass of Pedro Ximénez makes a great sweet finish. Pour about 50ml per person into small glasses and either drink straight or pour over vanilla ice cream.

The basics of sherry

I'm evangelical about sherry and every time someone tries it for the first time after I've cajoled them into it, it makes me happy. Here's what you need to know to get into shez.

First, sherry is massively undervalued, so you'll be able to try new things without spending a fortune – the same can't be said for drinks like whisky or gin. Second, sherry is a type of fortified wine (which simply means that a little brandy-type spirit is added to it in the barrel) from the southern Spanish towns Sanlúcar de Barrameda, El Puerto de Santa María and Jerez de la Frontera. 'Sherry' is the anglicised version of Jerez. If you ask for a 'sherry' in Spain you'll get a funny look.

Saying 'I don't like sherry' having tried it once years ago is ridiculous. Try it again and this time, try it properly – served at the right temperature (really cold for the light, dry styles, room temperature for the darker, sweeter sherries) and in the right-size glass (not a 'sherry glass' like the one Dot Cotton might serve the vicar 'a small sherry' in – a small wine glass is preferable).

Sherry needs food and food needs sherry. They make each other better. A bone-dry Fino will make your mouth salivate; partner it with some salty snacks or heavily savoury things like olives and marinated white Spanish anchovies and you're in pre-dinner heaven.

Sherry runs the full gamut from bone dry (drier than the driest white wine you've ever tried) and light (look for Fino or Manzanilla on the label) all the way through to the syrupy sweet and intensely dark, rich Pedro Ximénez (nearly always shortened to PX). As a rule, the lighter and drier sherries need to be drunk faster (a bottle, once opened, should be kept in the fridge and finished within a few days, just like a bottle of regular white wine) and the sweeter, darker sherries are OK stored at room temperature and don't need to be polished off so fast. These ones also tend to be a bit more expensive, so it's good to know you can buy a bottle and use it over a few weeks or months.

In the middle of the spectrum are all sorts of interesting things (look for Amontillado (amber coloured, medium-dry), Oloroso (dark gold, mellow, slightly sweeter), and Palo Cortado (in between) and they all go with different sorts of food. However, remember that the thing about food and wine matching is that different combos work for different people and although there are some classic matches with sherry (Fried Things And Fino is my restaurant concept dream), you might decide to drink Fino throughout your meal rather than just at the start, for example. You might like to crack open the PX with cheese rather than wait until afterwards. Do whatever you like and experiment. Here's to discovering sherry and trying new things. Salud!

Romantic dinner for two when you're just sussing each other out

Homemade pickles (and crisps)

This pickle recipe and method can be used for all types of vegetables. I had three kinds of cauliflower and wanted to keep their colours distinct so I bottled them separately. Feel free to mix stuff up, but beware that if beetroot is involved everything will turn pink. This recipe will make two jars each of the different varieties of cauliflower.

Makes 6 x 200ml jars

—

6 bay leaves
60g raw beetroot, peeled and
    cut into thin wedges
140g white cauliflower, cut into
    small florets
180g purple cauliflower, cut into
    small florets
180g green romanesco cauliflower,
    cut into small florets
3 garlic cloves, peeled and
    finely sliced

For the pickling brine
300ml white wine vinegar
300ml apple cider vinegar
300ml water
1½ tsp sugar
1½ tbsp flaked sea salt
2 tsp pink peppercorns
2 tsp allspice berries
1 tsp pul biber (mild Turkish
    chilli flakes)

Start by sterilising the jars. Wash 6 × 200ml Kilner jars and the lids in very hot, soapy water. Rinse thoroughly and then, being careful not to put your fingers anywhere near the lip or insides of the jars, sit them right way up on a baking tray and dry them out in a low oven (110–120°C/230–250°F/Gas mark ¼–½) for about 20 minutes. Remove them and fill while still warm.

Put all the pickling brine ingredients into a saucepan over a medium heat, bring to a simmer, stir and continue to simmer for 5 minutes. Remove the pan from the heat, cover and leave to cool.

Put a bay leaf in each of the 6 jars. Continue to assemble by putting the beetroot and white cauliflower together into 2 jars, the purple cauliflower into another 2 jars, and the green romanesco into the last 2 jars. Pickling separately will help the veg to keep their colour. Pour the brine evenly between the jars, distributing the spices equally. Seal with the lids. Their flavour will develop over the next few weeks and months. I suggest leaving them for at least 3 weeks before trying. Once open, keep them in the fridge.

Crisps

I absolutely love crisps. You can't have people over without them. That's part of entertainment law. Pick whatever ones you like best and quiz your new beau on their top crisp picks. This is essential info from a new partner. Personally, as the pickles are pretty strongly flavoured, I'd go for a quality plain crisp. Sea salt is all we need here.

DIY bruschetta bar AKA table picnic

Rosie's romesco

There are loads of ways of making the classic Catalan romesco sauce but my mate Rosie Birkett's is the best. This recipe is from her brilliant book *A Lot on Her Plate*, where she suggests serving it with grilled spring onions, but I love it piled on to toast, contrasting with the cool labneh.

25g roasted hazelnuts
25g blanched almonds
1 garlic clove, peeled
200g jarred roasted red
    peppers, drained
½ tsp tomato purée
60g stale sourdough bread
40ml extra-virgin olive oil
big pinch of cayenne pepper
big pinch of hot smoked paprika
1–2 tsp red wine vinegar
flaked sea salt and freshly ground
    black pepper

Put the nuts into a food processor with the garlic and blitz until you have coarse crumbs. Add the roasted peppers and blitz again to a coarse paste, then add the tomato purée, bread and a glug of the oil to loosen the mixture and blitz once more until you have a smoother paste. Pour the sauce into a bowl and season with flaked sea salt, black pepper, the cayenne pepper and paprika. Pour in the rest of the olive oil, stirring vigorously to incorporate it. Add the vinegar a little at a time until the sauce has the right acidity.

Baked toasts

4 small slices of good-quality bread
    per person, sourdough preferably
2 tsp extra-virgin olive oil
flaked sea salt and freshly
    ground black pepper

Preheat the oven to 180°C/350°F/Gas mark 4.

Drizzle both sides of the bread with olive oil. Lay on a baking tray and put in the centre of the oven for 5–10 minutes until golden, being careful not to take it too far. Sprinkle with flaked sea salt and black pepper before serving.

Herbed labneh

You can flavour labneh with all sorts of things. Loads of different herbs work well — in fact I can't really think of any that wouldn't. This is a good time to use up bits and pieces, and feel free to add in other flavours. Lemon zest and capers would work well too.

2 tbsp roughly chopped flat-leaf
    parsley leaves
1 tbsp roughly chopped mint leaves
½–1 tsp red or green fresh chilli,
    deseeded and finely chopped
1 tsp freshly squeezed lemon juice
1 tbsp extra-virgin olive oil
1 pinch of ground cumin
4 heaped tbsp Labneh (see recipe
    pages 92–3), or shop-bought
    cream cheese

Blitz up the parsley, mint and chilli with the lemon juice, oil and cumin. Put the labneh or cream cheese on a small plate. Use the back of a teaspoon to create a wiggly channel through it, then pour the herby oil into the grooves.

Pesto or Green Harissa

Any sort of pesto would be fine — homemade (see recipe, page 52) or a good-quality shop-bought pesto. Just tip it into a small bowl rather than bringing the jar to the table (unless it's a really posh one, then definitely bring it to the table). There's also a great walnut and basil pesto recipe in my first book that you should try if you haven't yet.

The Green harissa on pages 138–9 would also be delicious here.

Cheese from the deli

Head to your local deli and pick a few nice bits for your date-night spread. Don't go too mad, a couple of top-quality cheeses is infinitely preferable to a massive selection of crappy stuff. Personally, I'd go for a really good blue (my favourite is Beenleigh Blue), and a mature Cheddar – something like Westcombe. Remember you'll have the labneh too, so the soft side of things is taken care of.

Celeriac and golden beetroot remoulade

A classic celeriac remoulade is one of my favourite salads. I think this is even better. The walnuts give it a Waldorfy vibe. In fact, some apple matchsticks would be a lovely addition too. Whatever you do, don't grate the veg or use a food processor. You need to do this by hand. A good chance to practise your knife skills.

3 tbsp mayonnaise
1½ tbsp Greek-style yoghurt
1½ tbsp Dijon mustard
1½ tsp freshly squeezed lemon juice
3 raw golden beetroots
½ medium celeriac
30g walnuts
1½ heaped tbsp finely chopped
    flat-leaf parsley
flaked sea salt and freshly
    ground black pepper

In a large bowl, whisk together the mayonnaise, yoghurt, Dijon and lemon juice. Season well with flaked sea salt and black pepper and put to one side.

Peel the golden beetroots and celeriac and cut both into thin slices, then into fine matchsticks. As you prepare the veg, tip it straight into the dressing to stop it turning brown.

Toast the walnuts in a dry pan over a medium heat for 1–2 minutes until golden brown, shaking the pan often. Add to the veg with the parsley and toss everything together.

Individual tiramisu

There are all sorts of ways of making tiramisu, one of my all-time favourite desserts. This is my way. Easy, quick and delicious. These really benefit from resting before eating so that all the layers really get to know each other well and the whole thing soaks together. Make them the day before if you like, but definitely at least 4 hours before you want to eat them.

1 free-range egg, separated
30g caster sugar
30ml single cream
150g mascarpone
100ml strong coffee, cooled (made by putting 2 heaped tbsp freshly ground coffee in a cafetière with 140ml boiling water)
1 tbsp Marsala
1 tbsp dark rum
6 sponge fingers
2 tsp cocoa powder, for dusting

In a bowl, beat the egg yolk hard with the caster sugar using a rubber spatula until thick and mousse-like. In a separate bowl, whisk the cream and mascarpone with a balloon whisk until smooth. You don't want lumps. Add the egg yolk mixture to the mascarpone and beat well.

In a separate, clean bowl whisk the egg white to stiff peaks, then carefully fold into the mascarpone mixture. Put to one side. Have ready 2 small tumblers or wine glasses.

In a shallow bowl, mix together the coffee, the Marsala and the rum. Add the sponge fingers to the bowl, leave for 30 seconds, then flip over and leave until they have soaked up all of the liquid.

Now you are ready to start layering up. Put a spoonful of the mascarpone mixture at the bottom of each glass, then a quarter of the coffee-soaked biscuits, breaking them up to fit the shape of your glass. You need to use approximately 1½ fingers in the first layer of each glass. Add another spoonful of the mascarpone mixture evenly over the fingers in each glass, sprinkle with a generous amount of cocoa powder, then repeat, finishing with a layer of mascarpone mixture. Use the back of a teaspoon to create a swirl on the surface then, using a fine sieve, dust liberally with cocoa powder until totally covered. Leave to chill for at least 4 hours before serving.

Seared sea bream with
brown shrimps and watercress
in a chipotle butter_228

Green bean salad with
soft herbs, toasted walnuts,
shallots and feta_228

Bread and butter_229

Vanilla ice cream, candied
nuts and maple syrup_230

Dinner for two when you need to eat now and there's no time for prep

Seared sea bream with brown shrimps and watercress in a chipotle butter

2 fillets of sea bream
50g butter, plus extra for frying
1 tsp olive oil
½–1 level tsp chipotle chilli flakes
45g brown shrimps (leftover shrimps freeze really well)
2 big handfuls of watercress, large stalks removed
flaked sea salt and freshly ground black pepper

This simple fish dish is ready in a matter of minutes and only uses two pans, meaning minimal washing up. The quick dinner dream.

Wipe the fish fillets dry with kitchen paper and season with flaked sea salt and black pepper on both sides. Heat a knob of butter in a frying pan with the olive oil. Fry the fish fillets skin-side down first for about 1 minute until the skin is crispy, then flip over and turn off the heat.

In a separate pan melt the 50g butter. Add the chipotle chilli flakes, then throw in the shrimps and the watercress. Give everything a quick stir so the watercress starts to wilt and the shrimps are warmed through. Divide between 2 plates and top with the fish fillets.

Green bean salad with soft herbs, toasted walnuts, shallots and feta

4 tsp olive oil
1 tsp sherry vinegar
10g shallots, sliced into very fine rings
160g green beans, trimmed
20g walnut pieces
a sprig each of dill, mint, flat-leaf parsley and tarragon, leaves picked
40g feta cheese
flaked sea salt and freshly ground black pepper

Warm beans, soft herbs, cool feta, toasted nuts. A simple and delicious combination.

Put the oil, vinegar and a little flaked sea salt and black pepper in a serving bowl and whisk to combine. Add the shallot and keep to one side.

Bring a saucepan of water to the boil over a medium-high heat, add a large pinch of flaked sea salt, add the beans and cook for 4 minutes. Meanwhile, toast the walnuts in a dry pan over a medium heat for 1–2 minutes until golden brown, shaking the pan often.

After the beans have been cooking for 4 minutes, drain and immediately add to the dressing in the bowl. Add the herbs and toss well. Taste for seasoning. Crumble the feta over the beans and top with the toasted walnuts.

Bread
and butter

Your favourite bread and your
favourite butter. Your choice.
Just pick the good stuff.

Vanilla ice cream, candied nuts and maple syrup

Any leftover candied nuts will keep in an airtight tin or jar for a month. Nibble them with coffee and chocolate truffles, or serve like this...

Preheat the oven to 150°C/300°F/Gas mark 2.

Line a baking tray with foil and grease with a little vegetable oil.

Mix the sugars, cinnamon and chilli powder in a bowl. In another bowl, whisk the egg white to soft peaks, add the nuts and toss well to coat. Sprinkle the dry ingredients over the nuts with a large pinch of sea salt and mix everything together really well.

Spread the nuts out on the lined baking tray, making sure they are in a single layer. Bake for 40 minutes, stirring with a metal spoon halfway through cooking. They'll look really weird at this point. Don't panic. Leave to cool and harden. Sprinkle with a little more flaked sea salt before serving with ice cream and maple syrup.

For the candied nuts
vegetable oil, for greasing
50g caster sugar
35g soft dark brown sugar
1 tsp ground cinnamon
pinch of chilli powder
1 free-range egg white
175g mixed nuts (cashew nuts, walnuts, pecan nuts and almonds is the best combo)
flaked sea salt

To serve
vanilla ice cream, as much as you like
maple syrup, as much as you like

Weekend brunch for four people with slightly sore heads

Shezza
Bezza
Mary

This is my mate Ben's recipe. He is an absolute cocktail don and always comes up with incredible ideas for the menu at his place, Poco. He often uses seasonal fruit, foraged bits and homemade liqueurs. Here, we can forage from the local shops and whip up an easy weekend combo. Enjoy.

This makes a fresher version of a Bloody Mary but feel free to use 600ml of just tomato juice or beetroot juice if you like.

200ml vodka
400ml beetroot juice
200ml tomato juice
25ml freshly squeezed lemon juice
15 shakes of Worcestershire sauce
12 shakes of Tabasco, preferably
    smoked
100ml Fino sherry
½ tsp table salt
¼–½ tsp freshly ground
    black pepper
½ tsp celery salt
plenty of ice

To garnish
4 celery sticks, leaves intact
1 raw candy-stripe beetroot,
    sliced very finely
1 pinch of smoked paprika
1 pinch of sumac

Put everything, except the ice and garnishes, into a jug and stir well. If you can, leave it for half an hour before serving (ha ha, yeah right, like that's going to happen).

When you are ready to serve, give the mixture a good stir and adjust as necessary. Fill 4 glasses with ice cubes, pour over the mixture and garnish each glass with a celery stick, a slice or two of beetroot, a pinch of smoked paprika and a pinch of sumac. Serve with the smoked Tabasco and the Worcestershire sauce at the table so people can add more if they like.

Veggie haggis one-pan fry-up

500g vegetarian haggis
300g potatoes, halved or
    quartered if large
olive oil
8 chestnut mushrooms, sliced
1 large knob of salted butter
4–8 free-range eggs, depending
    on how hungry you are
big handful of watercress
flaked sea salt
HP sauce, to serve

I made this breakfast for my friends Cissy and Andy in their Edinburgh home the morning after we'd been out for a brilliant dinner with lots of wine and woke up feeling a little less than brilliant. It worked a treat and filled us all up for hours. Veggie haggis is easy to find in supermarkets. I used the Macsween variety. I recommend cooking the haggis and potatoes the day before for speed in the morning.

Cook the haggis according to the packet instructions. If you have a microwave this is very quick. If you don't (like me), you need to do it in the oven, which takes a while. The haggis will burst as it cooks but that's fine, as you crumble it up later anyway.

Put the potatoes in a saucepan, cover with cold water and a pinch of flaked sea salt, place over a high heat, bring to the boil, then lower the heat to medium and cook for 10–12 minutes until tender. Drain in a colander and leave to steam dry.

In your largest frying pan, heat some olive oil over a medium heat and fry the mushrooms for 5 minutes until golden on both sides. Tip onto a plate and set aside.

Return the pan to a high heat, add the butter with a splash more olive oil and once melted, fry the cooked potatoes until golden. I like plenty of crunchy bits but you will only achieve this if you don't move the potatoes around too much. Leaving them to sit in a pan over a high heat will result in some delicious crispy chunks.

When the potatoes are done, push them to one side. Crumble in the haggis and stir-fry for a few minutes. Make a gap and tip in the mushrooms. In a separate pan, fry the eggs in a little oil over a medium heat, then place them on top of everything in the pan and garnish with watercress. Let everybody help themselves from the pan. Serve with tea and HP Sauce.

Chocolate and coconut flapjacks with tea

So this is my thinking; if you make a tray of these before the weekend (say Thursday night), you can have them for Breakfast Pudding (definitely a thing) with another cup of tea after the haggis fry-up. Then, you could take some with you if you go for a walk. Then, you could have another bit on Sunday afternoon on the sofa. Then, probably have another bit on Sunday evening. Basically, flapjack all weekend. Yes please.

Makes 16

—

160g salted butter, plus extra for greasing
15g coconut flakes
100g caster sugar
50g golden syrup
200g rolled oats
20g Rice Krispies
30g salted and roasted peanuts, roughly chopped

For the topping
50g dark chocolate
2 tsp desiccated coconut
15g salted and roasted peanuts, roughly chopped

Preheat the oven to 170°C/325°F/Gas mark 3. Grease a 20 x 25cm baking tin with butter and line with greaseproof paper.

Toast the coconut flakes in a dry pan over a medium heat until golden, shaking the pan often. Set aside. Melt the sugar, butter and syrup together in a medium saucepan over a medium-low heat then, when totally melted, stir in the oats. Add the Rice Krispies, toasted coconut flakes and peanuts. Mix well, then tip into the lined tray. Roughly spread out with the back of your spoon, then lay a piece of cling film over the surface and use your hands to really carefully flatten and compress the mixture, right into the corners. You want the surface to be completely even and flat.

Peel off the cling film and bake in the hot oven for 20–22 minutes until golden brown. Leave to cool, then break the chocolate into chunks and melt in a bowl set over a pan of simmering water. Once melted, drizzle half the chocolate over the surface, sprinkle over the desiccated coconut and the peanuts, then finish with the remaining chocolate. Place on a wire rack to cool and set before cutting into 16 squares and serving. These flapjacks will keep well in a sealable container for 4 days.

Family lunch
for six –
eat your greens
or there's
no pud

Carla's tomatoes – pomodori a mezzo

I learnt how to make this classic Jewish-Roman tomato dish from Carla Tomasi – the most incredible Italian chef who is now back living in Rome after spending years working in London restaurants. A hugely experienced and knowledgeable cook, she is also calm and warm and the best teacher to learn from. The day I spent with her cooking in Rome was one of my faves ever and following her on Instagram (@carla_tomasi) is a joy. She is a master at preserving the seasons and generously shares pictures of everything she's cooking.

olive oil
6 ripe tomatoes
1 tsp caster sugar
1 tsp dried oregano
a few sprigs of thyme or rosemary
    (or both), leaves picked and
    finely chopped
2 garlic cloves, peeled and very
    finely sliced
2 tbsp fresh breadcrumbs
flaked sea salt

Preheat the oven to 180°C/350°F/Gas mark 4.

Drizzle the base of a 20 x 25cm ovenproof dish with 1 teaspoon of olive oil. Halve the tomatoes and sit them cut-side up in the dish. Sprinkle over the sugar, 1 teaspoon of flaked sea salt, the herbs, the garlic, then the breadcrumbs and finish with another drizzle of oil.

Bake in the hot oven for 30 minutes, then brown under a hot grill for a further 5. You can serve these hot, warm or cold, squished into a sandwich, as a side dish or stirred through pasta. They will keep well in the fridge in a sealable container for a couple of days.

As an optional extra, dot with soft goat's cheese once the tomatoes are out of the oven.

Fusilli with broccoli, spinach, basil and lemon

This easy pasta dish takes 30 minutes from start to finish, including waiting for the water to boil at the start. It's absolutely packed with green veg, is really filling and leftovers are delicious cold. The perfect midweek dinner or easy weekend lunch.

500g fusilli
700g broccoli, broken into florets, stalk peeled and sliced into ½cm discs
50g salted butter
2 garlic cloves, peeled and crushed
1 tsp pul biber (mild Turkish chilli flakes)
1 lemon, zested and juiced
125g baby spinach
1 large handful of basil leaves
60g Parmesan cheese, finely grated
3 tbsp extra-virgin olive oil
flaked sea salt and freshly ground black pepper

Bring a large saucepan of water to the boil over a high heat. Add two big pinches of flaked sea salt followed by the pasta. Bring back to the boil, stir once, then turn the heat down to medium and set a timer for 6 minutes.

When the timer goes off, add the broccoli to the pasta water and set the timer for another 4 minutes. Meanwhile, melt the butter in a small frying pan over a medium heat, add the garlic, pul biber and lemon juice and cook for 1–2 minutes until golden, stirring often, then remove from the heat.

When the timer goes off, try a piece of pasta to check that it's cooked, then drain the whole lot in a colander, reserving a little of the cooking water. Tip the cooked pasta and broccoli back into the saucepan, then add the baby spinach, the basil and the lemon zest. Stir well and cover with a lid. Give the garlicky butter a gentle stir, then pour over the pasta too. Add the Parmesan and a little of the cooking water to loosen if needed and season well with plenty of black pepper. Cover and give the whole pan a good shake while holding the lid down with a tea towel.

When you remove the lid, the Parmesan should have melted and everything should look delicious. If it looks a little dry, add some more of the pasta water and give it another shake. Drizzle over some extra-virgin olive oil and season to taste with salt and pepper. Take the pot to the table and let everybody serve themselves.

Parmesan panko courgette chips with green harissa dip

These 'chips' are baked, not fried, so you don't need to get the deep fryer out. Learning how to breadcrumb things like this (the technique is known as *paner* – 'to coat in breadcrumbs' in French) is a great basic skill, and can be applied to all sorts of things. Once you start, you won't stop. By sitting the breadcrumbed courgettes on a cooling rack instead of straight on a baking tray, you're giving them an extra chance of getting mega-crispy. These really need something good to dip them into. My favourite is the Green harissa (see recipe, pages 138–9). Mayo also works well.

2 medium courgettes
70g plain flour
2 free-range eggs
60g panko breadcrumbs
20g Parmesan cheese, finely grated
1 tsp dried oregano
Green harissa (see recipe,
    pages 138–9), for dipping
flaked sea salt and freshly ground
    black pepper

Preheat the oven to 220°C/425°F/Gas mark 7 and set a wire rack over a baking tray.

Cut the courgettes into batons approximately 10cm long. Tip the flour into a large freezer bag and season really well with a big pinch of flaked sea salt and black pepper. Add the courgette fingers to the bag, seal it and shake well.

Crack the eggs into a shallow bowl and beat them well. In a second shallow bowl, combine the panko breadcrumbs with the Parmesan and oregano.

Line up the bowls from left to right: your bag of floured courgettes, the beaten egg and the cheesy herby breadcrumbs. One at a time, remove the courgette sticks from the flour, shake off the excess and drop into the egg. Using your other hand (so you don't get egg in the breadcrumbs and vice versa), toss the courgette batons in the egg and then drop into the panko. Shake the bowl so that the courgettes are evenly covered in breadcrumbs and sit them on the wire rack, skin side down. Repeat until all the courgette batons have been egged and breadcrumbed. Bake for 15–20 minutes until golden brown.

Spiced plum and soured cream upside-down cake

See recipe, pages 160–61.

INDEX